~World of Dance~

Ballet

SECOND EDITION

World of Dance

~World of Dance~

Ballet

SECOND EDITION

Robin Rinaldi

Consulting editor:
Elizabeth A. Hanley,
Associate Professor
Emerita of Kinesiology,
Penn State University

Foreword by
Jacques D'Amboise,
Founder of the National
Dance Institute

CHELSEA HOUSE
PUBLISHERS

An imprint of Infobase

World of Dance: Ballet, Second Edition

Copyright © 2010 by Infobase Publishing

Chelsea House
An imprint of Infobase Publishing
132 West 31st Street
New York NY 10001

Library of Congress Cataloging-in-Publication Data
Rinaldi, Robin.
 Ballet / by Robin Rinaldi. — 2nd ed.
   p. cm. — (World of dance)
 Includes bibliographical references and index.
 ISBN 978-1-60413-479-7 (hardcover)
 1. Ballet--Juvenile literature. I. Title. II. Series.

GV1787.5.R55 2010
792.8—dc22   2009033611

Chelsea House books are available at special discounts when purchased in bulk quantities for businesses, associations, institutions, or sales promotions. Please call our Special Sales Department in New York at (212) 967-8800 or (800) 322-8755.

You can find Chelsea House on the World Wide Web at
http://www.chelseahouse.com

Text design by Kerry Casey
Cover design by Alicia Post
Composition by EJB Publishing Services
Cover printed by Bang Printing, Brainerd, MN
Book printed and bound by Bang Printing, Brainerd, MN
Date printed: February 2010
Printed in the United States of America

10 9 8 7 6 5 4 3 2 1

This book is printed on acid-free paper.

All links and Web addresses were checked and verified to be correct at the time of publication. Because of the dynamic nature of the Web, some addresses and links may have changed since publication and may no longer be valid.

CONTENTS

6 BALLET

INTRODUCTION

The world of dance is yours to enjoy! Dance has existed from time immemorial. It has been an integral part of celebrations and rituals, a means of communication with gods and among humans, and a basic source of enjoyment and beauty.

Dance is a fundamental element of human behavior and has evolved over the years from primitive movement of the earliest civilizations to traditional ethnic or folk styles, to the classical ballet and modern dance genres popular today. The term *dance* is broad and, therefore, not limited to the genres noted above. In the twenty-first century, dance includes ballroom, jazz, tap, aerobics, and a myriad of other movement activities. The joy derived from participating in dance of any genre and the physical activity required provide the opportunity for the pursuit of a healthy lifestyle in today's world.

The richness of cultural traditions observed in the ethnic, or folk, dance genre offers the participant, as well as the spectator, insight into the customs, geography, dress, and religious nature of a particular people. Originally passed on from one generation to the next, many ethnic, or folk, dances continue to evolve as our civilization and society change. From these quaint beginnings of traditional dance, a new genre emerged as a way to appeal to the upper level of society: ballet. This new form of dance rose quickly in popularity and remains so today. The genre of ethnic, or folk, dance continues to be an important part of ethnic communities throughout the United States, particularly in large cities.

When the era of modern dance emerged as a contrast and a challenge to the rigorously structured world of ballet, it was not readily accepted as an art form. Modern dance was interested in the communication of emotional experiences—through basic movement, as well as uninhibited movement—not through the academic tradition of ballet masters. Modern dance, however, found its aficionados and is a popular art form today.

No dance form is permanent, definitive, or ultimate. Changes occur, but the basic element of dance endures. Dance is for all people. One need only recall that dance needs neither common race nor common language for communication; it has been, and remains, a universal means of communication.

The WORLD OF DANCE series provides a starting point for readers interested in learning about ethnic, or folk, dances of world cultures, as well as the art forms of ballet and modern dance. This series features an overview of the development of these dance genres, from a historical perspective to a practical one. Highlighting specific cultures, their dance steps and movements, and their customs and traditions underscores the importance of these fundamental elements for the reader. Ballet and modern dance—more recent artistic dance genres—are explored in detail as well, giving the reader a comprehensive knowledge of the past, present, and potential future of each dance form.

The one fact that each reader should remember is that dance has always been, and always will be, a form of communication. This is its legacy to the world.

***

In this volume, Robin Rinaldi examines the theatrical dance known as ballet. This dance form developed within the royal courts of Italy and France during the sixteenth century, but did not flourish until two centuries later, when Jean-Georges Noverre's treatise *Lettres sur La Danse, et sur Les Ballets* stressed the importance of natural movements and gestures—which are augmented by music, costumes, and scenery—and that dancers convey stories. Among the most famous story ballets are *Swan Lake* and *The Nutcracker*, which have captivated audiences for more than a century.

—Elizabeth A. Hanley
Associate Professor Emerita of Kinesiology at
Pennsylvania State University

FOREWORD

In song and dance, man expresses himself as a member of a higher community. He has forgotten how to walk and speak and is on the way into flying into the air, dancing. . . . his very gestures express enchantment.
—Friedrich Nietzsche

In a conversation with George Balanchine (one of the twentieth century's most famous choreographers and the cofounder of the New York City Ballet) discussing the definition of dance, we evolved the following description: "Dance is an expression of time and space, using the control of movement and gesture to communicate."

Dance is central to the human being's expression of emotion. Every time we shake someone's hand, lift a glass in a toast, wave good-bye, or applaud a performer—we are doing a form of dance. We live in a universe of time and space, and dance is an art form invented by human beings to express and convey emotions. Dance is profound.

There are melodies that, when played, will cause your heart to droop with sadness for no known reason. Or a rousing jig or mazurka will have your foot tapping in an accompanying rhythm, seemingly beyond your control. The emotions, contacted through music, spur the body to react physically. Our bodies have just been programmed to express emotions. We dance for many reasons: for religious rituals from the most ancient times; for dealing with sadness, tearfully swaying and holding hands at a wake; for celebrating weddings, joyfully spinning in circles; for entertainment; for dating and mating. How many millions of couples through the ages have said, "We met at a dance"? But most of all, we dance for joy, often exclaiming, "How I love to dance!" Oh, the JOY OF DANCE!

I was teaching dance at a boarding school for emotionally disturbed children, ages 9 through 16. They were participating with 20 other schools in the National Dance Institute's (NDI) year-round program. The boarding school children had been traumatized in frightening and mind-boggling ways. There were a dozen students in my class, and the average attention span may have been 15 seconds—which made for a raucous bunch. This was a tough class.

One young boy, an 11-year-old, was an exception. He never took his eyes off of me for the 35 minutes of the dance class, and they were blazing blue eyes—electric, set in a chalk-white face. His body was slim, trim, superbly proportioned, and he stood arrow-straight. His lips were clamped in a rigid, determined line as he learned and executed every dance step with amazing skill. His concentration was intense despite the wild cavorting, noise, and otherwise disruptive behavior supplied by his fellow classmates.

At the end of class I went up to him and said, "Wow, can you dance. You're great! What's your name?"

Those blue eyes didn't blink. Then he parted his ridged lips and bared his teeth in a grimace that may have been a smile. He had a big hole where his front teeth should be. I covered my shock and didn't let it show. Both top and bottom incisors had been worn away by his continual grinding and rubbing of them together. One of the supervisors of the school rushed over to me and said, "Oh, his name is Michael. He's very intelligent, but he doesn't speak."

I heard Michael's story from the supervisor. Apparently, when he was a toddler in his playpen, he witnessed his father shooting his mother; then, putting the gun to his own head, the father killed himself. It was close to three days before the neighbors broke in to find the dead and swollen bodies of his parents. The dehydrated and starving little boy was stuck in his playpen, sitting in his own filth. The orphaned Michael disappeared into the foster care system, eventually ending up in the boarding school. No one had ever heard him speak.

In the ensuing weeks of dance class, I built and developed choreography for Michael and his classmates. In the spring, they were scheduled to dance in a spectacular NDI show called *The Event of the Year*. At the boarding school, I used Michael as the leader and as a model for the others and began welding all of the kids together, inventing a vigorous and energetic dance to utilize their explosive energy. It took awhile, but they were coming together, little by little over the months. And through all that time, the best in the class—the determined and concentrating Michael—never spoke.

That spring, dancers from the 22 different schools with which the NDI had dance programs were scheduled to come together at Madison Square Garden for *The Event of the Year*. There would be more than 2,000 dancers, a symphony orchestra, a jazz orchestra, a chorus, Broadway stars, narrators, and Native American Indian drummers. There was scenery that was the length of an entire city block and visiting guest children from six foreign countries coming to dance with our New York City children. All of these elements had to come together and fit into a spectacular performance, with only one day of rehearsal. The foremost challenge was how to get 2,000 dancing children on stage for the opening number.

At NDI, we have developed a system called "the runs." First, we divide the stage into a grid with colored lines making the outlines of box shapes, making a mosaic of patterns and shapes on the stage floor. Each outlined box holds a class from one of the schools, which consists of 15 to 30 children. Then, we add various colored lines as tracks, starting offstage and leading to the boxes. The dancers line up in the wings, hallways, and various holding areas on either side of the stage. At the end of the overture, they burst onto the stage, running and leaping and following their colored tracks to their respective boxes, where they explode into the opening dance number.

We had less than three minutes to accomplish "the runs." It's as if a couple of dozen trains coming from different places and traveling on different tracks all arrived at a station at the same time, safely pulling into their allotted spaces. But even before starting, it would take us almost an hour just to get the dancers lined up in the correct holding areas offstage, ready to make their entrance. We had scheduled one shot to rehearse the opening. It had to work the first time or we would have to repeat everything. That meant going into overtime at a great expense.

I gave the cue to start the number. The orchestra, singers, lights, and stagehands all commenced on cue, and the avalanche of 2,000 children were let loose on their tracks. "The runs" had begun!

After about a minute, I realized something was wrong. There was a big pileup on stage left and children were colliding into each other and bunching up behind some obstacle. I ran over to discover the source of the problem: Michael and his classmates. He had ignored everything and led the group from his school right up front, as close to the audience as he could get. Inspiring his dancing buddies, they were a crew of leaping, contorting demons—dancing up a storm, but blocking some 600 other dancers trying to get through.

I rushed up to them, yelling, "You're in the wrong place! Back up! Back up!"

Michael—with his eyes blazing, mouth open, and legs and arms spinning in dance movements like an eggbeater—yelled out, "Oh, I am so happy! I am so happy! Thank you, Jacques! Oh, it's so good! I am so happy!"

I backed off, stunned into silence. I sat down in the first row of the audience and was joined by several of the supervisors, teachers, and chaperones from Michael's school, our mouths open in wonder. The spirit of dance had taken over Michael and his classmates. No one danced better or with more passion in the whole show that night and with Michael leading the way—the JOY OF DANCE was at work. (We went into overtime, but so what!)

—Jacques D'Amboise
Author of *Teaching the Magic of Dance*, winner of an
Academy Award for *He Makes Me Feel Like Dancin'*,
and Founder of the National Dance Institute

The Human
Body as Art

Dance is the only art in which we ourselves are the stuff of which it is made.

—dancer and choreographer Ted Shawn

Whether it was a Christmas performance of *The Nutcracker*, a television performance of *Swan Lake*, or a class we took as a child, most of us have been exposed, on some level, to ballet. Yet, you may still wonder: What is ballet, and what is so unique about this form of dance that seems so graceful and orderly?

All ballet is dance, but not all dance is ballet. Ballet is a very specific and prescribed sort of dancing. Dance has existed almost as long as humans have walked the Earth, but ballet is only 400 years old. Anyone can put on some music, move his or her body to its rhythm, and call it dancing. However, it takes years to train a body into the relatively few positions that make up ballet's vocabulary of steps. Dance can be performed in the street, in a house, in a school gymnasium—basically anywhere. A ballet, however, only takes place in a theater, or at least on some sort of stage. Many people teach themselves to dance, but virtually

13

nobody can learn ballet the way some teach themselves to act, paint, sing, or play guitar. It must be learned in a school under the tutelage of a highly trained teacher.

Ballet is the most academic form of theatrical dance, and the most difficult to learn and perform. Most professional dancers—not only ballerinas but Broadway performers and modern dancers as well—have been trained in ballet as a foundation. Gymnasts and figure skaters often study ballet, too. National Football League coaches have even been known to send their players to ballet class for strength training.

Ballet is the most academic form of theatrical dance and takes dedication to achieve success. Here, male and female ballet dancers extend their arms while posing in midair, showing their strength and flexibility.

Ballet dancers are fond of quoting Edward Villella, one of the top male dancers of the twentieth century and a former welterweight boxing champion, who concluded that it took as much physical strength to dance a three-minute *pas de deux* as it did to go a three-minute round of boxing. Of course, there are differences. A boxer can grunt, sweat, frown, bleed, fall down, and generally let the audience witness his effort. A ballet dancer, however, has to pull off similar feats of strength and agility while smiling and seeming to fly through the air gracefully and effortlessly.

TURNOUT, THE FIVE POSITIONS, AND THE VOCABULARY OF STEPS

The basis of ballet, and its primary difference from all other forms of dance, is what dancers call **turnout**: the positioning of the legs and feet in a 180-degree line at all times. In other words, instead of standing normally with the feet facing forward, they are "turned out" into a straight line with the toes pointing away from each other. Turnout begins in the hip socket, so that the knees as well as the toes face outward. It takes many years of practice to develop.

Ballet dancers must keep their feet and legs constantly turned out. Plus, they must also begin and end each step from one of five basic positions, conveniently labeled *first, second, third, fourth,* and *fifth position*. (See the Glossary for explanations.)

Moreover, the movements a dancer performs onstage (and in class as well) are—at least in strictly classical ballet—limited to a few hundred specific steps that were invented centuries ago in France and have been passed down from teacher to pupil through the years. Because there are only so many words in the English language, a speaker cannot simply invent words. Similarly, a ballet dancer cannot just invent a step. He or she must use the existing steps and perform them according to established standards that, depending on the particular teacher or **choreographer**, can be quite precise. This goes for every movement performed with legs, arms, and torso, right down to the tilt of the head and the angle of each finger.

To make things even more complicated, all the steps are still in French. This holds true whether the ballet class is being held in China, Russia, Egypt, or Spain. When the teacher or choreographer says *plié*, the dancer bends his or her knees. When *relevé* is uttered, the dancer springs up on his or her toes. Hearing *jeté*, the dancer leaps forward. This repertoire of French steps is just one of the aspects that have made ballet seem a rigid, old-fashioned art not easily understood or appreciated by the average person.

THE RIGORS OF BALLET TRAINING

When considering turnout, the positions of the feet, and the fixed set of steps that comprise the foundation of ballet, it is not hard to imagine the kind of training it takes to become a professional ballet dancer. Both genders, but especially females—who must learn to dance *en pointe*, or on the tips of their toes—begin ballet classes by age 10 because it takes many years to mold the body into the unnatural shapes ballet demands.

Many parents send their children to ballet class as a hobby, and for most it ends there, perhaps culminating in a role in an annual production of *The Nutcracker*. Even so, some ballet training during childhood yields many benefits, including poise, increased flexibility that can last well into adulthood, physical confidence, and often a lifelong appreciation of music and other performing arts.

Some of these students—those who possess inborn talent, a good physique, and a passion for ballet—will end up taking more and more classes. The few who are serious about becoming professionals will go on to audition at a prestigious ballet school, many of which are affiliated with ballet companies, or at a performing arts high school that focuses as much on dance as it does on academics.

From these schools, many dancers are then picked to join professional ballet companies, some as young as 16. Others major in dance at four-year colleges before auditioning for companies. The dancers who

A group of young dancers in Seattle prepare to audition for the Pacific Northwest Ballet's performance of *The Nutcracker*. Children typically start attending ballet classes well before age 10 because it takes several years to develop the physical skills necessary to achieve success.

make it to this level have typically been training for at least 10 years; if they are female, they have been *en pointe* since about age 12. Most of them will need the preferred ballet physique: average height with long, lean limbs and muscles that are well defined but not bulky.

Once a dancer joins a professional company, the real work begins. An average schedule might include an hour-and-a-half morning class, a few hours of rehearsal, an afternoon class, some physical therapy if there are injuries to work on, and other forms of strength training such as Pilates or Nautilus. If the company is currently in performance, the day also includes either a matinee or nighttime performance. Most professional dancers work about 12 hours a day, six days a week.

Not surprisingly, ballet careers rarely extend long past the age of 40. By then, a dancer's strength and agility are declining, though in relation to the general population, the dancer is still amazingly strong and flexible. At this point some dancers retire, but most go on to become teachers and choreographers in their own right, training the next generation of students.

(continues on page 20)

THE NUTCRACKER

Choreography by Lev Ivanov, 1892
Music by Pyotr Ilyich Tchaikovsky

The most popular and best-known ballet in the United States is based on a nineteenth-century German fairy tale, "The Nutcracker and the Mouse King," by E.T.A. Hoffman. The two-act ballet begins at Christmastime in the home of Dr. and Mrs. Stahlbaum, who are hosting a holiday party. As elegantly dressed couples arrive with their children, we meet the Stahlbaums' daughter, Clara (in some productions called Marie), the story's protagonist. A charming and dreamy girl, Clara is elated when her godfather, the

Dancers perform the "Waltz of the Snowflakes" during the first act of *The Nutcracker*. The most popular ballet in the United States, *The Nutcracker* appeals to audiences with its fairy tale story, wide variety of dances, and well-known music by Tchaikovsky.

mysterious toymaker Drosselmeyer, appears in his black cape. Drosselmeyer enchants the children with life-sized dancing "toys" and then presents Clara, his favorite, with her Christmas gift: a soldierlike Nutcracker doll, which Clara adores but which, unfortunately, falls into the hands of her mischievous brother Fritz, who promptly breaks it and receives a scolding. After Drosselmeyer bandages the "wounded" doll and consoles Clara, the party disperses, and darkness descends on the Stahlbaum house.

Clara soon returns to the stage in her nightdress, searching for her Nutcracker under the Christmas tree and drifting off to sleep with the doll in her arms as the clock strikes midnight. Now Clara's dream begins to unfold onstage. Huge mice scurry in, terrifying her, and close on their heels comes their leader, the evil Mouse King. As Tchaikovsky's music increases in tempo and volume, the furniture in the room flies away, and the Christmas tree grows to a gigantic height (special effects that generally delight the children in the audience). The Nutcracker comes to life and so do an entire army of toy soldiers, who fend off the mice while the Nutcracker duels the Mouse King. Just when it seems the Nutcracker will be defeated, Clara throws her shoe at the Mouse King, distracting him long enough for the Nutcracker to make the kill.

Again, the scene changes, and Clara finds herself alone with the Nutcracker, who has magically come to life in the form of a young prince. He leads her on a journey through the Kingdom of the Snow, where snowflakes (the **corps de ballet** dressed in white tutus) begin dancing around them along with the Snow Queen and King. Here, the mood changes dramatically from a character-driven story ballet with much pantomime to a more classical, dance-centered work. The Snow Queen and King perform a lyrical and

(continues)

(continued)

dramatic *pas de deux*, which closes the first act as Clara and her Nutcracker prince make their way onward to the Kingdom of Sweets.

Act II opens in this kingdom, a candyland of sorts, ruled by the Sugarplum Fairy—the ballet's star. At her command, a host of delicacies—chocolate from Spain, tea from China, coffee from Arabia, and several others—come forward one by one to dance for the young travelers in a series of ethnically flavored **divertissements**. At the culmination, the Sugar Plum Fairy dances a **grand pas de deux** with her cavalier, and then the Kingdom's inhabitants wave goodbye to Clara and the Nutcracker as they continue their journey—usually disappearing into the sky in a balloon.

The Nutcracker's appeal can perhaps be explained by the fact that it can be enjoyed on so many levels. Its fairytale quality, the liveliness of Act I, and the short varietal dances in Act II make it a favorite of children, who stand in line by the thousands each fall to audition for regional productions across the country. Its music, including the "Waltz of the Flowers" and the "Dance of the Sugarplum Fairy," stands on its own as favorite Christmas music, and serious ballet aficionados enjoy the ballet's lovely group and solo dances throughout the second act and in the Kingdom of the Snow.

(continued from page 17)

For unlike other performing arts such as music, opera, and theater, ballet's standards and repertoire are, by and large, not written down. Instead, they are passed down orally from teacher to students. Thus, great teachers and choreographers are highly revered in the ballet world and considered as important as, or even more important than, the dancers themselves.

WHAT IS IT ALL ABOUT?

One might wonder why dancers devote themselves to such a regimen. Unlike many musicians, actors, and singers, ballet dancers never earn much money, and their careers are fairly short. A dancer in his or her prime is much like an Olympic athlete in constant training—there is not much time for a social life, a family, or outside interests.

Obviously, ballet dancers share the same dedication to their art as do painters, poets, and composers. Its difficulty only makes it more of a challenge and a greater achievement once a dance or a role is mastered. Ballet demands more than just physical prowess and athleticism, because its main goal is not simply for the performer to jump high or spin quickly but also to communicate an emotion or idea and to do so with undeniable beauty.

That is what turnout is all about. It is not just an arbitrary quirk that somehow caught on and has been passed down to today's dancers. Turnout allows the dancer to move his lower body in much more varied ways, especially from side to side on stage, while providing the audience with a profile view of his or her legs and feet. Its angularity bestows a rarefied, crystalline look.

Beauty, and a certain dignity of form, are also at the root of ballet's vocabulary of steps, most of which portray either long, straight lines extending high and away from the body, as in *arabesque*; graceful arcs and circles, as in **attitude** and *pirouette*; or the illusion of flight, as in *grand jeté* and *bourée*. These patterns are inherently symmetrical and visually pleasing, even to the untrained eye.

All of these steps are like the colors on an artist's palette. Choreographers "paint" the steps onto the dancers to create a kind of moving canvas. Each dancer is the medium, as well as the artist—each one has his or her own unique skills, personality, and expression. Ballet has been likened to sculpture or poetry that is actually alive with movement.

Then there is the music, an integral element of ballet—so integral, in fact, that the great choreographer George Balanchine defined ballet simply as "music personified." Ballet dancers, choreographers, and admirers are usually music lovers, and if they do not start out that way, they certainly acquire a deep appreciation of music

Through their many and varied steps, ballet dancers illustrate the symmetry of their bodies. Here, a ballerina holds onto a barre while extending her leg in an *arabesque* pose.

gained by the added dimension of "dancing out the score," whether it be an orchestral symphony, a modern composition, or even pop or rock music.

The subject matter of most ballets, too, heightens the emotions of both performers and audiences. The first ballets portrayed ancient gods and myths; later, many romantic ballets were based either on classic tales such as *The Sleeping Beauty* and *Romeo and Juliet* or on spiritual topics such as death, the afterlife, and forgiveness. Today, ballets deal with every subject imaginable—from primal experiences, such as love, longing, and sexuality, to political and social statements about racism, violence, and war. The combination of music, movements, and nonverbal acting creates a deeply emotional experience. Performing or watching a ballet often brings feelings of catharsis, sadness, and joy—sometimes all at once. The dancers' finely honed techniques and almost superhuman athleticism only add to the experience.

As the dancer Mikhail Baryshnikov explained in Robert Greskovic's *Ballet 101: A Complete Guide to Learning and Loving the Ballet*, ballet "has to do with the great blessings and disasters that are the center of our lives, the things one is usually too embarrassed or too frightened to talk about. There they were . . . in crystallized form."

Ballet Begins
in Europe

When discussing the history of ballet, one must be sure to distinguish between social and folk dancing, which have existed in cultures throughout the world for thousands of years, and theatrical dancing, in which dancers perform for an audience. Early ballet was certainly influenced by the social dancing of its day—what would normally be called ballroom dancing. Although it often borrows ideas and movements from various folk dances, ballet is in essence a very specific kind of theatrical dancing.

The first seed of theatrical dancing was planted in ancient Greece, where song-and-dance celebrations in honor of the god Dionysus were part of Greek theater. The root of the English word *orchestra* is the Greek *orkestra*, which means "round dancing floor." The nine Muses—the goddesses who inspired artists of all kinds and are the root of our word *music*—included Terpsichore, muse of poetry and dance.

During the Dark and Middle Ages (about A.D. 410–1300), theater—along with many of the other arts and sciences in Europe—went into a period of stagnation as the Catholic Church rose to prominence and people became more concerned with survival in this world and salvation in the next. The Renaissance of the fifteenth and sixteenth centuries brought an awakening of interest in all things human and especially in reviving the arts of the ancient Greeks and Romans. This is when ballet was born.

THE EARLIEST COURT BALLETS

Ballet comes from the Italian word *ballo*, meaning dance, and in the Italian city-states of the fifteenth century, many *balli* (dances) were held. The aristocrats had the time and money to pursue and fund artistic endeavors. They hired dance teachers to instruct members of the court in the popular dances of the day, which were customary at the many galas thrown by the aristocracy—parties, weddings, and celebrations of all kinds. These *balli*, or court dances, involved very specific steps, but

Italian city-states, such as Turin, held *balli*, or court dances, as part of the festivities during the aristocracy's many annual galas. A scene from the ballet *Il Dono del Re Alpi à Madama Reale* is depicted in this scene with Turin in the background.

looked more like what would now be called ballroom dancing. Their patterns resembled those of today's figure skaters who trace circles and arcs across a large floor.

A new form of dance called *entrées* came about in the late 1400s. Today, we think of *entrées* as the courses of a meal, and that is just how these dances were "served up" to their royal audiences—usually between the courses of a long meal at wedding banquets. They were short dance

---

LE BALLET COMIQUE DE LA REINE (THE QUEEN'S BALLET SPECTACLE)

Choreography by Balthasar de Beaujoyeulx, 1581

Though generally regarded as the first court ballet, *Le Ballet Comique de la Reine* looked nothing like what we call ballet today. First, it was performed not on a proscenium stage but instead on the floor of a huge hall of France's royal palace, with the public sitting in two levels of galleries looking down on the action. Second, it included not only dances but also sung and spoken verses—as well as opulent scenery, such as chariots, floats, and fountains—in a sort of cross between ballet, opera, and theater. Third, the dancers were not trained professionals but instead amateur nobles, and all were male. *La Ballet Comique*—whose name does not imply a comical tone but rather a coherent dramatic theme, which previous court spectacles had lacked—was staged during the reign of King Henri III (Catherine de Medici's son) and his wife, Queen Louise, to celebrate the marriage of Louise's sister, Margaret of Lorraine, to the Duc de Joyeuse. As was

segments, or *divertissements*, performed solely by men wearing wigs, masks, and intricate costumes. They incorporated both poetry and singing into the dancing. To get an idea of how elaborately and seriously planned these entertainments could be, their décor, costumes, and stage machinery were often provided by the best artists of the time, including Leonardo Da Vinci.

(continues on page 30)

common back then, the marriage had a political purpose, to restore peace and strengthen the royal family's authority after many years of religious civil wars.

The ballet's plot managed to pay homage to the sovereign while employing classical Greek symbolism, which was much in vogue during the Renaissance. The main characters were Ulysses, the hero of Homer's *Odyssey*, and Circe, the sorceress who holds him hostage. With the king and queen seated front and center of the action, the ballet made them into passive but central characters in the plot, which begins when Ulysses throws himself at the foot of the king in an effort to escape Circe, begging the king to summon Peace and Harmony in order to free him from the evil witch. For the next six hours, all manner of mythological characters of the sea—sirens, tritons, naiads—sing, recite, and dance in intricate geometrical patterns such as squares, triangles, and circles, which themselves were thought to be symbolic and even magical. In the end, Ulysses finds that he cannot break free of Circe, who controls the cycle of the seasons and is, after all, a supernatural being. He must appeal to the gods Pan, Mercury, and Jupiter, who attack Circe's castle and take her prisoner. The ballet concludes with the goddess Athena paying honor to the queen. The performers then presented the royals with symbolic emblems.

LA BALLET DE LA NUIT (BALLET OF THE NIGHT)

Just as *Le Ballet Comique de la Reine* had at its core a political message regarding the strengthening of the royal crown after a period of upheaval, so, too, did *La Ballet de la Nuit*. The five years prior to its debut had seen a series of protests against the royal family perpetrated by France's judicial body, other nobles, and the middle class and peasantry as well. By 1653, the monarchy had regained control and was eager to retain it by casting the teenage king in as grand a light as possible.

Fortunately, 15-year-old Louis XIV was a talented and enthusiastic dancer. In *La Ballet de la Nuit*, a lengthy ballet set on a proscenium stage with 43 separate dances extending into the wee hours of the morning, he danced as several characters. The ballet takes as its subject the 12 hours of night beginning at 6 P.M. and ending at 6 A.M. or dawn. Its four scenes follow the course of the night: 6 to 9 P.M., 9 P.M. to midnight, midnight to 3 A.M., and 3 A.M. to sunrise. During the first scene, in early evening, the sun sets and characters such as bandits, gypsies, and vagabonds appear in a darkened, lawless quarter of the city. The second scene portrays the time of night reserved for fetes and ballets, featuring masquerades and pantomimes. The third scene brings out Egyptian astrologers and the Persian priest Zoroaster, who are enchanted by the Moon; when it goes into eclipse, the theme turns darker as thieves loot a burning house while families flee the fire. In the final scene, darkness gives way to dawn as Aurora appears with her 12 hours of day. Here Louis made his entrance as Apollo, god of the sun, the bringer of light, riches, victory, and peace. In a Roman-cut suit and headdress decorated in gilded "rays," Louis became known thereafter as the Sun King.

As a talented dancer, Louis XIV was largely responsible for making ballet such an important part of French culture. At the age of 15, the French king danced as several characters in *La Ballet de la Nuit (Ballet of the Night)*, including Apollo, depicted in this seventeenth-century painting.

(continued from page 27)

When the Italian noblewoman Catherine de Medici married into the royal family of France in 1533, she brought knowledge of *balli* with her to the French royal court. Catherine was a great admirer of dance and a renowned hostess as well. To celebrate a family member's marriage in 1581, she presented the *Le Ballet Comique de la Reine* (*The Queen's Ballet Spectacle*), a six-hour extravaganza of music, song, and dance that is known as the first ballet, or court ballet as it was called back then.

Many of the early court ballets were based on gods, goddesses, and classical myths; ordinary people and problems were seen as crude and below the realm of high art. *Le Ballet Comique de la Reine*, for example, played out scenes from the legendary Greek story of Ulysses escaping from the sorceress Circe as told in Homer's *Odyssey*. The term *comique* actually does not mean that the ballet was meant to be comedic or funny; a closer translation would be "theatrical" or "dramatic."

BALLET'S FOUNDING FATHERS: BEAUCHAMPS, LULLY, AND NOVERRE

Ballet got a big boost when Louis XIV ascended to the throne of France. The young king had been schooled in all of the courtly arts, such as fencing and music, but dance was arguably his favorite. At age 15 he danced the role of Apollo, the ancient Greek god of the sun, in *La Ballet de la Nuit* (*Ballet of the Night*), which bestowed on him the popular title of "Sun King" for the rest of his life.

Louis XIV took the art of dance seriously, establishing the Académie Royale de Danse in 1661, which employed 13 **ballet masters**, who are considered high-ranking teachers and choreographers. One of these was Pierre Beauchamps, who would go on to codify the five turned-out positions of the feet as well as many of the basic ballet steps still performed and still referred to solely in French today. Though even social or ballroom dancing favored a slight turnout to the feet, the development of the proscenium arch—the arch defining the front of a stage that separates the space between audience and performer—made turnout even more pronounced and important.

Early *balli* in France were performed in ballrooms, or what today would be called "in the round." Dancers sometimes performed on raised platforms and could often be viewed from many angles. When the Paris Opera stage changed from a palace ballroom to a proscenium arch in 1669, the relationship between dancer and audience underwent a historic shift. Now the audience could only view the dancer from one angle—the front—while he moved primarily from one side of the stage to the other. Turnout provided the best way to achieve this side-to-side movement and give the audience a profile view of his legs and feet, all while he was facing them.

Louis XIV also hired violinist, composer, and dancer Jean-Baptiste Lully as director of the Académie Royale de Musique, within which Lully established his own dance academy. Today, it is known as the Paris Opera Ballet, the oldest ballet academy in the world. From this academy, or *école de danse*, comes today's term *danse d'école*, or "dance of the school," meaning any dancing that honors the strict conventions and steps established for ballet during this time.

Another of ballet's founding fathers was Jean-Georges Noverre, also known as the "Shakespeare of dance." Instead of the court ballets that featured the aristocracy in elaborate, restrictive costumes, high heels, wigs, and masks, Noverre argued for a new kind of ballet that was more expressive and natural. He developed what is called the *ballet d'action*, the first kind of ballet to discard the use of songs or words and to depend entirely on dance, gesture, and pantomime set to music. Instead of short *divertissements* that could vary from subject to subject, the *ballet d'action* had a more coherent theme or plot. Noverre also encouraged dancers to discard their masks and lighten their costumes.

Noverre's ideas began to take root as he helped spread ballet throughout Europe. His career as a ballet master took him to Germany, England, Austria, and Italy throughout the 1700s. His *Lettres sur la Danse et sur les Ballets* (*Letters on Dancing and Ballets*) is one of the founding treatises on ballet, outlining his theories of *ballet d'action*—namely, that dance and dance alone could be its own art form and sustain drama, narrative, and emotion. With Noverre's help, in due course, the new art form began to be practiced by devoted professionals instead of aristocratic amateurs whose main goal was to throw a memorable party.

Depicted in this seventeenth-century painting, Italian-born Jean-Baptiste Lully was first a dancer for Louis XIV, and then, in the 1650s and 1660s, he composed several ballet scores for the king. In 1672, Louis XIV appointed him director of the Académie Royale de Musique.

WOMEN, COMMONERS, AND DEMOCRACY

In its first few centuries, ballet remained an art completely dominated by men. Then, in 1681, Lully brought the first female dancer, known only as Mademoiselle Lafontaine, to the Paris stage in *Le Triomphe de l'Amour* (*The Triumph of Love*). Though little is known of Lafontaine's life or training, her appearance made history, and with the arrival of the ballerina, there was no turning back—changes were under way.

As women began dancing in public, the costuming became more naturalistic and less confining, with the high heels of the court shed for soft, heelless slippers. Two of the first ballerinas were Marie-Anne de Cupis de Camargo, a **virtuoso** who dazzled audiences with her athleticism, and Maria Sallé, a more expressive and poetic dancer. The two women joined in ballet's first great rivalry, one that illustrated two aspects

Marie-Anne de Cupis de Camargo, shown here in this circa 1730 oil painting by Nicolas Lancret, was one of the first well-known ballerinas. The French–Belgian dancer made her debut at the Paris Opera Ballet in May 1726 and would go on to introduce many innovations to ballet, including heelless slippers and shortened skirts.

of dance—the technical versus the lyrical—that are still somewhat in competition today. Camargo scandalized the public by shortening her skirts' hemlines to above the ankle in order to show off her intricate footwork. Sallé did her bit to move things forward by abandoning the huge hoop skirts and wigs of the day for a muslin tunic, sandals, and her own loosened hair.

Around this time, England, which had been putting on its own court ballets since the early 1600s, joined France and Italy in the ballet craze when Sallé went to London in 1733 to perform *Pygmalion*,

LA FILLE MAL GARDÉE (THE ILL-WATCHED DAUGHTER)

Original choreography by Jean Dauberval, 1789; restaged by Frederick Ashton, 1960
Music by Ferdinand Hérold

The first *ballet d'action* to portray the lives and concerns of ordinary people as opposed to gods and goddesses, *La Fille* is the oldest ballet currently performed in the world. Set in the countryside of France, it tells the story of Lise, a young girl in love with the handsome, devoted Colas. The only problem is that Lise's mother, the Widow Simone, wants her to marry Alain, the simpleton son of a wealthy landowner. Though Lise keeps sneaking off to steal moments with her beau, Simone is never far behind, ready to yank her daughter back into the house at every turn. Full of playful innocence and comedic touches, *La Fille's* popularity rests on its bucolic setting, its charming mime sequences, its pastoral group dances, and, most of all, on the chemistry and dancing of its male and female leads,

depicting a statue brought to life by the Greek goddess Aphrodite. Ballet also took root in Russia when its empress, Anna Ivanovna, established the world's second ballet academy, the Imperial St. Petersburg School, in 1738. Though its name would change through the ages, becoming the Imperial Russian Ballet and later the Maryinsky (aka Kirov) Ballet, this school still produces many of the world's leading dancers.

As will be seen in subsequent chapters, ballet's history often was influenced by the political currents of the countries in which it developed. This was the case in the late 1700s on the eve of the French Revolution,

who must portray ardent young love without ever reaching into the territory of passion or sexuality (à la *Romeo and Juliet*).

Ribbons are used as a symbol of love throughout the ballet. One of its highlights is a dance in which Lise and Colas intertwine in a ribbon, spooling toward and away from each other and weaving the material into patterns between them. In another dance, Lise's girlfriends encircle and hold her *en pointe* via eight ribbons she holds above her head while they form a "wheel" around her, rotating her by moving in a circle as each holds the end of one ribbon. The ballet also includes folkloric touches in the form of a clog dance, a maypole dance, and a morris dance (an English folk dance for men). Hérold's score is by turns lively and lyrical, and there is some serious technical dancing for the two leads, each performing precise feats of *batterie* (leg beats in the air) and some stunning turns, as well as lovely, graceful **adagios** (slow, lyrical dances).

In the end, of course, Simone gives her approval, and Lise and Colas are allowed to marry; this propels the whole happy village into a finale in which the lovers are celebrated. *La Fille* is the ballet version of an entertaining sitcom or a "chick flick"—light, romantic, and entertaining.

which would overthrow France's royal house and ultimately establish a democracy in its place; ballet also began to illustrate this shift. Instead of taking the ancient gods or the splendor of the aristocracy for its subject matter, ballet began to focus more on common themes, ordinary characters, and natural settings. The year 1789 brought *La Fille Mal Gardée* (*The Ill-Watched Daughter*) to the stage, which told a quaint story about the lives and loves of French peasants living in the countryside. It became wildly popular and has become the oldest ballet that is still regularly performed today.

Even though commoners who were becoming skilled professionals took up ballet, and even though its themes began to revolve around ordinary life, it is easy to see that the refinement and sophistication of Europe's royal courts forever marked ballet at its conception. The delicacy and dignity that still make ballet seem to many a "high art" are a legacy of the French and Italian aristocrats who gave ballet its start.

The Romantic Period

By the early 1800s, art and literature's Romantic periods were well underway. The Romantics glorified humankind's emotional and spiritual dimensions while spurning the strictly scientific and intellectual view of the world, which they regarded as cold and inhuman. The effects were felt in the dance world and, combined with a few coincidences, led to a full flowering of ballet's own great Romantic period.

The first important event was the emergence of Italian-born ballerina Marie Taglioni. Her father, Filippo, who was a ballet teacher, constructed the first Romantic ballet, *La Sylphide*, in 1832 primarily to showcase his daughter's talents. The story of a nymph (a female spirit of the woods, which would become a staple character in many ballets) who lures a young Scotsman away from his daily life and into the forest, *La Sylphide* marks several turning points in ballet. These milestones included the emergence of a large female *corps de ballet* backing up the lead ballerina, the lightening of the standard feminine costume to a long tulle skirt, the focus on naturalistic and spiritual topics, and, most important, the beginning of dancing *en pointe*. Pointe dancing, as much as turnout and the five positions, exemplifies ballet and is now the standard for all ballerinas. At the time of its introduction, however, audiences were enthralled to see Taglioni balancing on her tiptoes throughout the ballet, not only because of the physical demands it required but also because of the ethereal, lyrical quality it brought to the stage, presenting an image of Taglioni almost ready to lift off into flight.

Today, *pointe* shoes (or **toe shoes**, as they are often called) are blocked—that is, the area surrounding the toes is greatly stiffened with extra material and glue beneath its shiny satin exterior. Ballerinas sometimes use soft padding or lambs' wool inside their shoes to cushion the effect of the toes hitting the floor repeatedly. Even so, a look at any ballerina's foot makes clear the strains of pointe dancing; the toes are frequently bruised and blistered, toenails often blackened or missing—a far cry from the dainty view of the shoed foot seen by the audience.

In Taglioni's time, however, the modern point shoe had not been invented, so the only support for the ballerina came from darning the slippers' toes to reinforce and thicken the material there, making the dancers' achievement all the more impressive. For a time, French choreographer Charles-Louis Didelot helped his ballerinas balance on their toes—as well as fly through the air—with the aid of stage machines that hooked the dancers to wires. By the time of *La Sylphide*, Taglioni was balancing on her toes unaided by props.

If Taglioni was the first great **prima ballerina**, the second one followed closely on her heels—or toes. While "La Taglioni" was gliding across stages in her flowing white skirt, Fanny Elssler was displaying another strain of Romanticism in Paris in *Le Diable Boiteux* (*The Devil on Two Sticks*). Set in Spain, the ballet featured Elssler doing her *cachuca*, a balletic rendition of a traditional stomping, passionate Spanish dance featuring castanets. Comparisons between the earthy, sensual Elssler and the heavenly, refined Taglioni soon became the talk of Europe, and ballet's second great female rivalry was born.

In more technical terms, the two ballerinas embodied two very different but essential characteristics of ballet. Taglioni displayed exemplary *ballon*—the ability to jump seemingly with ease and, for a moment, to even hover in the air. A modern (though not balletic) example of someone with terrific ballon is former NBA star Michael Jordan. Elssler, on the other hand, perfected the art of *terre à terre*—a dance in which the feet barely leave the ground but which still expresses a fiery, sexy appeal.

Featured in this color print of *La Sylphide*, Marie Taglioni was an Italian–Swedish ballerina who became one of the most famous performers of the Romantic ballet era. *La Sylphide* was specifically created by her father, Filippo, to showcase her talent for performing *en pointe*, or on the tips of her toes.

THE *CORPS DE BALLET*

It was not only the great soloists who emerged into the spotlight during the Romantic era. Ballets such as *La Sylphide*, and later *Giselle*, *La Bayadère*, and *Swan Lake*, all feature climactic scenes in which the lead male is lured into a mystical kingdom—be it a forest, a midnight lake, or some sort of underworld—where he confronts his mistress among her kind, a large group of women who are not fully human. These "ballet blancs," as they were called because of the sheer white (*blanc* in French) costumes worn by the women, were the first to showcase an integral part of classical ballet: the *corps de ballet*, the company's crew of female dancers whose function was to dance in unison behind the soloist.

During the nineteenth century, the *corps de ballet* (meaning "body of ballet") emerged to serve as a backdrop to the soloists during performances. In this modern illustration of a *corps de ballet*, dancers from the Ukrainian National Ballet perform *Swan Lake* behind the soloists, Odette and Prince Siegfried, at the Odessa Opera House.

Although a prima ballerina exults before the audience in feats of balance, multiple turns, and high leaps, it is the corps' job to typically form a vision of lyrical harmony, with every arm moving at exactly the same angle and every leg pointed in exactly the same direction. In the best *corps de ballets*, no one dancer stands out either physically or technically. Their job is to blend into one unified whole; timing and control are their specialties.

Today's *corps de ballets* include both genders, and in some companies they are used as centerpieces in and of themselves, not only as a backdrop to the soloists. The ballet blanc sections of the Romantic ballets, however, remain the realm of the female corps and often provide as many emotional and technical highlights as do the featured solos, albeit of a different kind. The "Dance of the Cygnets" in *Swan Lake* is a prime example of a group dance of amazing precision and timing; so, too, is the sight of dozens of dancers waving their arms gracefully in unison, creating a mesmerizing illusion of birds in flight.

PETIPA'S FORMULA FOR CLASSICAL BALLET

Although the first production of *La Sylphide* took place in Paris and the most famous ballerinas of the day continued to emerge from Italy, the second half of the nineteenth century saw the axis of the ballet world shift from Western Europe to Russia. Yet, it was a Frenchman who was largely responsible for this.

As the grand ballet master of the Imperial Russian Ballet (today known as the formidable Maryinsky, aka Kirov, Ballet), Marius Petipa created five of ballet's greatest classics in the late nineteenth century—*Don Quixote*, *La Bayadère*, *The Sleeping Beauty*, *Swan Lake*, and *The Nutcracker*—as well as restaged *Giselle* and *Coppélia*.

All of Petipa's masterworks share common traits that mark them as the underpinnings of what is now regarded as the classical repertoire. For narratives, they take either the romantic idea of a man lured to an otherworld by a spirit-woman (as in *La Bayadère* and *Swan Lake*) or

(continues on page 44)

GISELLE

Original Choreography by Jules Perrot and Jean
    Coralli, 1841; restaged by Marius Petipa, 1884
Music by Adolphe Adam

Giselle is the quintessential Romantic ballet in both its theme—which centers on the physical world versus the afterlife, and on revenge versus forgiveness—and in its look, which gives us long white tulle skirts (as opposed to the more modern short **tutus**) and a "ballet blanc" for a second act. Giselle is a role that requires great dramatic skill as well as virtuosic dancing from its lead ballerina; Carlotta Grisi made the role famous at the 1841 premiere of the ballet, and today, it is requisite dancing for any accomplished ballerina.

The story is set in a German village, where the maiden Giselle lives with her mother. Though frail, Giselle loves to dance, and Act I features many lovely displays of her skill. When a nobleman, Count Albrecht, enters the village disguised as a peasant, he and Giselle fall in love. Following the tradition of many great ballets, operas, and plays, it is love at first sight and soon Albrecht has sworn himself to Giselle. A hunting party of other nobles—among them Albrecht's friends and actual fiancé, Bathilde—appear, and Albrecht's ruse is unmasked. Giselle, betrayed and wracked with grief, has a breakdown in a famous "mad scene" that has her tearing at her hair, nearly stabbing herself, and finally collapsing into the arms of her mother, dead.

Act II opens in a dark forest, where Giselle is buried. Soon, female spirits called Wilis, veiled and dressed in white, appear in a mournful promenade of hauntingly identical *arabesque*. Based on vampirelike, dancing female spirits in Slavonic folklore, the Wilis are the ghosts of women who have died before their wedding day, and they will kill

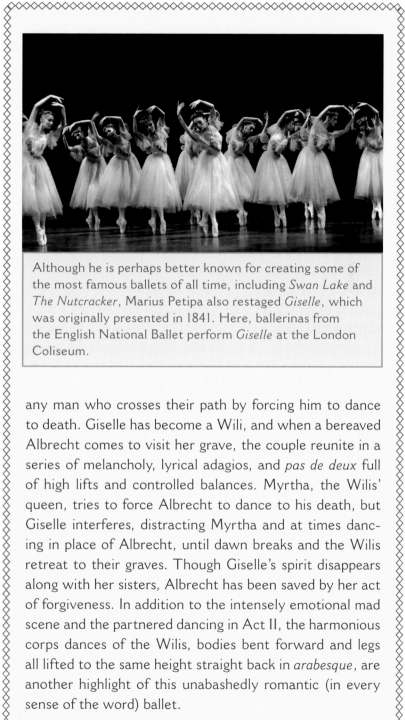

Although he is perhaps better known for creating some of the most famous ballets of all time, including *Swan Lake* and *The Nutcracker*, Marius Petipa also restaged *Giselle*, which was originally presented in 1841. Here, ballerinas from the English National Ballet perform *Giselle* at the London Coliseum.

any man who crosses their path by forcing him to dance to death. Giselle has become a Wili, and when a bereaved Albrecht comes to visit her grave, the couple reunite in a series of melancholy, lyrical adagios, and *pas de deux* full of high lifts and controlled balances. Myrtha, the Wilis' queen, tries to force Albrecht to dance to his death, but Giselle interferes, distracting Myrtha and at times dancing in place of Albrecht, until dawn breaks and the Wilis retreat to their graves. Though Giselle's spirit disappears along with her sisters, Albrecht has been saved by her act of forgiveness. In addition to the intensely emotional mad scene and the partnered dancing in Act II, the harmonious corps dances of the Wilis, bodies bent forward and legs all lifted to the same height straight back in *arabesque*, are another highlight of this unabashedly romantic (in every sense of the word) ballet.

(continued from page 41)

traditional works of literature and fairy tales (as in *Don Quixote*, *The Sleeping Beauty*, and *The Nutcracker*). They generally begin with group dances in a character or folkloric vein, with much pantomime used to put the story in motion, and then proceed to a pivotal dream or ballet blanc sequence featuring the lead ballerina and her corps. The last act of the ballet usually culminates with a variety of dances not particularly tied to the plotline; the setting of these *divertissements* is often the wedding celebration of the hero and heroine, but in reality they are just artistic excuses to showcase the dancers' finesse with differing styles. Finally, the ballet climaxes with the *grand pas de deux*, a Petipa invention recognized as the ballet standard the world over.

The grand pas de deux, which translates simply as "big step for two," begins with an *adagio* (slow, lyrical dance) between the male and female dancer, marked by supported high **extensions** of the woman's legs, multiple *pirouettes* (a kind of one-legged spin) aided by the man's guiding hand above the woman's head or at her waist, and acrobatic lifts of the woman over the man's head. This is followed by an **allegro** (a quick, lively combination) by the male dancer showcasing his ability to leap and spin, an allegro for the ballerina featuring light footwork and pirouettes, and a **coda** (or finale) that reunites them in an exuberant flourish.

The dramatic action of the opening scenes, the corps' presentation of the dreamy ballet blancs, the *divertissements* showing a range of ethnically tinged styles, and the *grand pas de deux* are what audiences of classical ballet have come to expect in a full-length piece. Petipa put this formula in place and added the last necessary element: great music.

Up until Petipa's time, most ballet music was given only secondary consideration to the dancing. The Russian composer Pyotr Ilyich Tchaikovsky changed that. By composing scores that were complex and symphonic as well as danceable, he added another dimension of beauty to the art. His scores for *Swan Lake*, *The Sleeping Beauty*, and *The Nutcracker* are famous compositions even for non-balletgoers. *Tchaikovsky's* music and Petipa's choreography brought ballet to new heights and secured Russia's place in the history of classical ballet.

THE THREE SCHOOLS OF CLASSICAL BALLET

Not only did Romantic classical ballet develop during the nineteenth century, but it was also during this time that three distinct styles, or schools, of ballet technique began to be recognized and consciously passed down through structured teaching systems, published books, and, as always, directly from teacher to student.

The French School

The oldest, the **French School** was the original basis for ballet as developed in the court of Louis XIV by ballet masters such as Beauchamps and Noverre, as previously discussed. Known for its grace and elegance rather than its technical virtuosity, the French School was nevertheless held in high regard. While the Russians were soaking up every last detail of French technique under Petipa in the late nineteenth century, French ballet itself was undergoing a period of stagnation. During this time, Parisian audiences were entirely male, and they seemed much more interested in carousing backstage with the all-female casts than in watching them from the audience. Many famous paintings by Edgar Degas capture the look and feel of French ballet during this time.

The Italian School

Known for its dexterity, difficulty of its steps, high leaps, and multiple turns, the **Italian School** was largely the creation of Carlo Blasis, who became director of the Imperial Dancing Academy in Milan in 1837. Blasis did the ballet world a huge service when he wrote down all that was known about the dance's structure in two books, *An Elementary Treatise upon the Theory and Practice of the Art of Dancing* and *The Code of Terpsichore*. Blasis's technique was passed down through his pupil Giovanni Lepri to Enrico Cecchetti, a brilliant dancer, teacher, and mime artist who brought the athletic Italian style to Russia in 1887, where he stunned audiences and went on to become a legendary teacher. He

(continues on page 49)

SWAN LAKE

Choreography by Marius Petipa and Lev Ivanov, 1895

Music by Pyotr Ilyich Tchaikovsky

Perhaps the best-known and most popular of the classical ballets, *Swan Lake* serves as an example of Marius Petipa's formula: an introductory group scene that sets the action in motion; a dream sequence or ballet blanc; and a culminating party scene or gathering of the original group of characters, with several *divertissements* inserted for variety, crowned by a *grand pas de deux*. It is all set to the symphonic accompaniment of the great composer Tchaikovsky. *Swan Lake*'s female lead switches from a swan queen named Odette in Act II to an evil impersonator named Odile in Act III. The same ballerina dances both roles. The ballet ends with a short fourth act.

Based on a German folktale, the ballet has a first act set in the court of Prince Siegfried. It is his birthday, and his mother, the Queen, presents him with the gift of a crossbow while reminding him that his time has come to choose a bride. Though he dances with several women, he remains distracted, even melancholy, and when the party-goers leave (after performing various group waltzes and a *pas de trios*, or "dance for three"), he takes his crossbow to a nearby lake to hunt.

Act II opens on the moonlit lake, where the prince sees swans flying; he aims his crossbow. Suddenly, a swan appears before him in the form of a woman-creature—Odette, the Swan Queen—who flutters her "wings" nervously. The evil magician Baron von Rothbart has cursed Odette. By day, she and her fellow maidens are swans; between midnight and dawn they resort to women, watched

Some of the more experienced members of a company's *corps de ballet* are featured in performances such as the "Dance of the Cygnets" in *Swan Lake*.

over by von Rothbart in the guise of an owl. The curse can only be broken by a man's sincere pledge of love. Among *Swan Lake*'s many charms are the flowing, birdlike movements of its star ballerina and corps, all dressed in white tutus and feathered head caps. The prince becomes enchanted with Odette, and Act II sees their *pas de deux* alternating with group dances of the corps of swans.

One of the most breathtaking is the "Dance of the Cygnets," in which four of the swans, arms intertwined and hands linked, dance in quick, perfect unison. The prince, of course, declares his love to Odette before dawn breaks, and she and her fellow maidens revert to swans and "fly" off. Here one sees some of the commonalities among the romantic ballets: *Giselle*'s Wilis return to their graves at

(continues)

(continued)

dawn, *Swan Lake*'s maidens return to bird form. Also, the story turns on a man's vow, which holds the power to either destroy a woman or liberate her from a miserable destiny—themes that run through *Cinderella* and *The Sleeping Beauty* as well.

Act III returns to the royal court, where Siegfried's mother again insists on his choosing a bride. For the betrothal festivities, dancers from Hungary, Poland, Spain, and Naples arrive—another of Petipa's conventions for showcasing a variety of national dances. Again, Siegfried is unimpressed with the six women presented to him as potential brides, but when a mysterious nobleman (von Rothbart in disguise) arrives with his daughter Odile—danced by the same ballerina as Odette, but in a black tutu and acting cunning and much livelier—the prince takes her for his beloved swan maiden. Amid the already full festivities, they dance a *grand pas deux* whose coda culminates in Odile performing 32 **fouettés**—quick turns done from one leg with the other whipping in and out. Siegfried pledges his troth to Odile, and in that moment von Rothbart reveals himself, victorious in his attempt to make the prince renounce his vow to Odette, who must now remain a swan forever.

Act IV returns to the lakeside where Odette is grieving over her betrayal by Siegfried. When he comes to her, penitent, to confess his mistake, the two decide to end their lives together and thus free themselves to unite in the afterlife. Though von Rothbart tries to stop them, the two dive into the lake, which breaks the curse, while the swan maidens gather to bid farewell to their queen and her lover, who are seen sailing off into the afterlife as von Rothbart perishes.

(continued from page 45)
developed his own regimented style of training involving very specific daily and weekly lesson plans, described in his book *A Manual on the Theory and Practice of Classical Theatrical Dancing.* The book is used to this day—particularly in England, where he later settled—to produce dancers of great technical strength.

The Russian School

The **Russian School** is a synthesis of the two other schools: the French, brought by Petipa and his forerunners, and the Italian, brought by Cecchetti. Thus, many consider its combination of serene elegance and breathtaking virtuosity the most complete and well-developed technique in all of ballet. Near the close of the nineteenth century, young Russian dancers were begging to be trained by Cecchetti. Through him one can trace not only the best dancers of the early 1900s—Anna Pavlova, Vaslav Nijinsky, and Michael Fokine—but also many students who went on to develop companies or teaching systems of their own, such as Agrippina Vaganova in Russia and Ninette de Valois in England.

During the early twentieth century, many of these magnificent dancers and teachers would take the Russian technique back to France and not only revitalize ballet for the next century, but also spread it from Europe throughout the world.

4

The Russians Bring Ballet to the World

If ballet's progress in the nineteenth century was marked by French dance makers such as Petipa and the French School of ballet taking root in Russian soil, then the twentieth century brought just the opposite: Native Russians took their training and creative vision to France—and then to the world. Although Petipa and others before him had worked to bring structure and narrative clarity to the nineteenth-century classics, the twentieth century began with a revolt against Petipa's classicism and a push for more natural, expressive ways of moving.

The modern ballet era began in 1909 in Paris when the Russian Serge Diaghilev—neither a dancer nor a choreographer but an arts enthusiast and impresario—introduced the Ballets Russes, a company whose influence, through the various choreographers and dancers it spawned, is still felt today. The history of the Ballets Russes reads like a roster of the greatest ballet figures of all time: Michael Fokine, Vaslav Nijinsky, Léonide Massine, Bronislava Nijinska, Anna Pavlova, Ninette de Valois, and George Balanchine—all of whom did their part to both spread the existing art form to the world and to modernize it. In addition to nurturing soon-to-be famous dancers and choreographers, Ballets Russes also became known for working with the premier artists and musicians of the time. Igor Stravinsky, Maurice Ravel, Claude Debussy, and Serge Prokoviev created scores for Ballets Russes, and artists such as Pablo Picasso, Henri Matisse, and Max Ernst devised sets.

One of Ballets Russes' most influential dancers and choreographers, Michael Fokine rejected Petipa's formula for the multiact classical ballet based on fairy tale and the afterlife; instead, he created shorter ballets with earthier, more folkloric themes and more passionate choreography, such as *The Firebird*, *Le Spectre de la Rose* (*The Spirit of the Rose*), *Petrouchka*, and *Scheherazade*. His ballets also gave more stage time to male dancers, something Parisian audiences had greatly missed in the late nineteenth century, when men had been relegated to sexually obsessed observers.

THE GREAT NIJINSKY AND "LA PAVLOVA"

One of these male dancers made an especially indelible impression with his fierce sensuality and heretofore-unseen technical strength. Vaslav Nijinsky, the star of many of Fokine's ballets, could not only leap higher and beat his legs faster than anyone before him, but he projected such charisma that he immediately became Ballets Russes' biggest star. As the Spirit in *Le Spectre de la Rose*, Nijinsky's costume of flower petals and fluidly melting limbs made him seem more plantlike than human; as the puppet come to life in *Petrouchka*, his half-human melancholy was palpable. As the Golden Slave in *Scheherazade*, his erotic and highly physical dancing raised eyebrows. His emotional and technical range seemed unlimited.

Although Nijinsky was an enormously gifted dancer, he is perhaps best known for two ballets he choreographed, which broke many dance and social barriers at the time. In 1912's *L'Après-midi d'un Faune* (*Afternoon of a Faun*, not to be confused with Jerome Robbins's 1953 ballet of the same name), Nijinsky took the flattened, angular poses seen in Greek art and used them to portray a primal scene come to life: a man-beast carousing with young nymphs of the forest. The sexual overtones and non-balletic movement of the piece caused scandal and sensation among Parisian audiences, but that was nothing compared to Nijinsky's creation the following year: a joyful praise of Russia's pagan history called *Le Sacre du*

Vaslav Nijinsky, who was of Russian and Polish descent, was renowned for his gravity-defying leaps and was one of the first male ballet dancers to perform *en pointe*. Here, he is in character as the faun in the ballet *Afternoon of a Faun* in Paris 1912.

Printemps (*The Rite of Spring*). In this ballet—or antiballet, as some might call it—dancers stomped heavily onstage as if engaged in a tribal rite celebrating the coming of spring. There were no pointe shoes, no delicate **pirouettes**, no chivalrous partnering—just a group of bodies moving pigeon-toed and animal-like to an ominous score by Igor Stravinsky, and the climax of the piece involves the sacrifice of a virgin. Brazenly ahead of its time and much too shocking for audiences to support, it played only seven performances and was not restaged until 75 years later.

Nijinsky's life was just as consuming offstage. He was Diaghilev's live-in lover for a time—an arrangement he claimed to have agreed to for the sake of his career and financial security. When he unexpectedly married while touring South America at the age of 24, Diaghilev was so furious that he fired Nijinsky, an event that marked the beginning of Nijinsky's descent into schizophrenia. In 1919, at the age of 30, he entered an institution and spent the rest of his life in mental hospitals throughout Europe. Unbeknownst to him, his work had been a harbinger of the modern dance movement that would soon begin in the United States.

Another star of the Ballets Russes who shone just as brightly, but much less controversially, was Anna Pavlova, a young ballerina who had been trained by both Petipa and Cecchetti in Russia. In fact, Cecchetti had devoted three years of his career solely to her training. Lithe, willowy, and utterly poetic in her dancing, Pavlova captivated audiences first in Russia, then in Paris, and finally worldwide when she began to manage her own career—an unheard-of feat for a female dancer before that time.

From 1911 until 1929, Pavlova toured the world, performing solos and abbreviated versions of the classics in many countries and on continents that had never before seen ballet, including Australia, Japan, India, South America, North America, South Africa, and New Zealand, where ballet companies began springing up soon after her legendary appearances. Pavlova's signature piece was *The Dying Swan*, a one-act ballet created by Fokine in which the ballerina portrayed a dying bird. A filmed performance still survives, though it is not commercially available. "La Pavlova," as she was affectionately known, almost singlehandedly spread ballet from its roots in Europe and Russia to the rest of the world. Her achievement would be mirrored a few decades later by Margot Fonteyn, a ballerina from England, where Pavlova eventually made her home.

ENGLAND'S ROYAL BALLET AND MARGOT FONTEYN

Pavlova's tireless touring and the far-flung synergy of Ballets Russes are also indirectly responsible for the flourishing of the ballet movement in

England. After the great ballet master Cecchetti worked with the company from 1909 to 1918, he moved to London, where one of his pupils, former Ballets Russes dancer Ninette de Valois, was working to establish a ballet company that would eventually be known as Britain's Royal Ballet.

For a choreographer, de Valois chose Frederick Ashton, a native Ecuadorian (born William Mallandaine) who developed a passion for

LE SACRE DU PRINTEMPS (RITE OF SPRING)

Choreography by Vaslav Nijinksy, 1913
Music by Igor Stravinsky

Rite of Spring, as it is commonly known even though Stravinsky himself called it "The Coronation of Spring," began with the composer's famous score, upon which Nijinsky's choreography was built. The music—discordant, nonmelodic, and thunderous—brought about its own revolution in the way classical music was perceived and composed. But since both the score and the ballet premiered together on a May night in Paris in 1913, the effect on the audience's senses was doubled.

In two acts, *Rite of Spring* basically takes the viewer back to an imagined, prehistoric Russia—which in many minds played out as a metaphor for the darkness of the human subconscious. Act I opens on a green hillside at the end of winter. Young women and men, dressed in heavy peasant robes, dance in groups, first lightheartedly and then more aggressively. At one point the men carry the women offstage, playing at abducting them, until a wise tribal elder with a long beard and tall hat enters and the youngsters become still. The act ends with the men dancing a frenzied ritual of earth worship.

dancing after seeing Pavlova perform in Peru. Although de Valois's company's name changed from the Vic-Wells Ballet to the Sadler's Wells Ballet and finally to the Royal Ballet, Ashton remained its primary choreographer for 35 years, helping define a lyrical style of dancing known for its suppleness and interesting curves and angles in the upper body.

The second act opens on a harsher landscape marked with sacred stones and framed by ox skulls hanging from poles. A group of tribal virgins encircles the stage and performs a magical dance, choosing one of their own to be sacrificed in the process. The chosen woman stands alone in the middle of the circle as the tribe gathers round her, the ancestors are summoned, and the whole tribe dances a violent, sacrificial rite until the chosen woman falls dead on the ground.

As if the subject matter weren't controversial enough in polite Paris society, Nijinsky's choreography—described as asymmetric, spasmatic, sluggish, larvalike, ugly—shocked audiences by presenting movements never before seen. Instead of turnout, the dancers' feet were turned in, with their legs knock-kneed. One dancer commented that, instead of aspiring to the lightness and grace typical of ballet, Nijinsky actually constructed the dance so that every movement actually caused physical pain, as if the dancers' bodies were being thrown heavily around the stage. The audience didn't quite know what to make of it all. Boos and jeers almost drowned out the orchestra, men came to blows, and outside the theater a riot erupted. Nijinsky, Stravinsky, and Ballets Russes impresario Serge Diaghilev were said to be despondent afterward. The ballet disappeared from the repertoire after just six more performances and was restaged 75 years later by the Joffrey Ballet in 1988.

Ashton's muse was British ballerina Margot Fonteyn, who had debuted at the Vic-Wells Ballet in 1935 at the tender age of 16. Though not an extremely athletic dancer, Fonteyn charmed audiences with her perfect balletic physique, pure and seemingly effortless **line**, and regal beauty, as well as the warmth of her characterizations. Ashton created some of the Royal Ballet's masterpieces around her, such as the plotless *Symphonic Variations* and

L'APRÈS-MIDI D'UN FAUNE (AFTERNOON OF A FAUN)

Choreography by Vaslav Nijinsky, 1912
Music by Claude Debussy

Nijinsky's first attempt at choreography, which shocked and scandalized Parisian audiences, was ironically based on the strains of Debussy's *Prelude a' L'Après-midi d'un Faune*, a soft, lulling piece of flute music that sounds more like the accompaniment to an idyllic picnic than an erotically charged ballet that broke with nearly every tradition. Taking his cue from the music, Nijinsky's main character (danced by himself) is a faun—a half-human and half-animal creature of the woods much like a satyr, or man-goat—who comes upon seven young nymphs in the forest. Unlike Debussy's gentle score, however, Nijinsky's faun is full of primal sexual energy as he attempts to mate with one of the nymphs, who drops a scarf as she flees from him. The ballet culminates with the faun alone, fondling her scarf and finally lying on top of it erotically, arching into a spasm of sexual delight. Not only did Nijinsky insert a sexual theme into what could have been an innocent pastoral interlude, his choreography also went in the opposite direction of ballet.

the story of the ethereal water sprite *Ondine*, and made her the centerpiece in many of the Royal Ballet's restagings of classics, such as *The Sleeping Beauty*.

Fonteyn's stellar career in England was only half of her story; in the 1960s she would team up with the greatest male dancer in the world, and together they would help spawn a worldwide dance boom, just as Pavlova had in the early 1900s.

Taking his visual inspiration from the bas-relief of Greek friezes, in which flattened characters stood in profile, Nijinsky eliminated toe shoes—he did not allow a pointed foot, let alone delicate arcs or curves. The dancers move about a shallow portion of the stage by way of a bent-kneed, flat-footed shuffle. Their faces never look at the audience but instead turn suddenly one way or another in profile with shoulders stiff, arms angled sharply, and hands having no space between the fingers. Surely, ballet had never before, or ever since, seen anything quite like it. Though the nymphs do exude a certain feminine grace—with arms linked as they shuffle first right and then left, changing direction without cue from the music—the faun's movements are more animalistic as his feet paw at the floor and he arches his pelvis far forward in attempting to join with the desired nymph. With *Faune*, Nijinsky, perhaps without realizing it, created the first modern dance. Though Isadora Duncan was improvising the beginnings of naturalistic, modern dance onstage during this same period, she created no formal choreography to hand down. Even so, *Faune* is categorized as a ballet, albeit a very new kind of ballet that broke all the rules and widened the thematic and structural scope of dance in one giant leap.

Russian ballerina Anna Pavlova, pictured in the early 1900s, was one of the most famous classical ballet dancers of her time. She is perhaps best known for becoming the first ballerina to tour the world and is also held in high esteem for originating the role of the Dying Swan, a solo ballet performance.

THE SOVIET REVOLUTION YIELDS BALANCHINE AND MORE

As if nurturing many of the century's greatest European dancers and choreographers were not enough, Ballets Russes also contained the seed of America's ballet future in the form of a young dancer named Georgi Balanchivadze, who left Soviet Russia in 1924 to join Diaghilev and his fellow dancers in Monte Carlo, where Ballets Russes had stationed itself after the Bolshevik Revolution of 1917.

As had happened before, international politics had far-reaching implications in ballet's history—namely, when czarist Russia became the Soviet Union, many of its dancers and choreographers fled under the strain of the new Socialist order. Ironically, the Communist Party actually lent its full support to ballet, funding it so generously that by mid-century, Moscow's Bolshoi Ballet would stun the world upon its first tour of the West. The "Russian method" of instruction also became prominent at this time under the auspices of Agrippina Vaganova. She was a student of Cecchetti's who remained in St. Petersburg (then Leningrad) after the Revolution, merging the finer points of the French and Italian schools into the "**Vaganova system**," as outlined in her book *Fundamentals of Classic Dance*.

When Balanchivadze arrived in France, Diaghilev quickly changed the young man's name to George Balanchine and asked him to begin choreographing new works for the troupe. This Balanchine did with great prolificness, creating eight ballets in as many years. Though he was trained as a dancer, it soon became clear that Balanchine's gift lay in choreography, and in 1928 he created *Apollo*, a portrayal of the youth of the Greek sun god, and the first of many Balanchine classics. *Apollo* is actually touted as the first "neoclassical" ballet, as Balanchine's work would come to be known—keeping the purity and form of classical ballet but stripping it of its elaborate storylines, mime, and heavy theatrics, thus resulting in a leaner, cleaner kind of classicism.

Balanchine might have gone on to create many more works for Ballets Russes, but the company that had become the trunk of so many branches on the tree of ballet collapsed upon Diaghilev's death in 1929.

Arriving in the United States in the fall of 1933, Russian-born choreographer George Balanchine would quickly make a name for himself in American ballet. Balanchine, who choreographed Broadway shows in the 1930s and 1940s, is pictured here with his wife, Vera Zorina (*front*), and other ballerinas in January 1935.

While others went on to restructure the troupe, Balanchine went in search of a new company to call his own. He got his chance in 1933, when Lincoln Kirstein, a wealthy American heir and ballet lover, made him an offer to come to the United States and establish his own company. Balanchine agreed, and thus was born what would eventually become the New York City Ballet, where Balanchine's neoclassicism could take root and flower into a uniquely American strain of ballet.

American Neoclassicism: The Balanchine Era

Where ballet is concerned, the United States is extremely lucky. The European art form with aristocratic beginnings had, for the most part, paid only occasional visits to America's shores. Americans proved to be a devoted audience, as witnessed during Fanny Elssler's 1840 tour, when the U.S. Senate recessed to mark her first performance in Washington, D.C. Although the United States had produced a few dancers and had seen the creation of professional companies in Philadelphia and San Francisco by the 1930s, the country undeniably entered ballet quite late in the game. When ballet did finally arrive in full force, anyone could have brought it from Europe. Instead of just anyone, however, America got George Balanchine, arguably the greatest ballet master of the century—and, some say, of all time. Balanchine's benefactor, Lincoln Kirstein, adored ballet, but knew very little about it. Thus, Balanchine was given free rein to create any kind of company he liked, and he ended up creating one quite different from anything that had existed before.

First came the school. In 1934, Balanchine founded the School of American Ballet and soon after created his first American work for its students—*Serenade*, a ballet without a story or a set, danced in simple costumes by a female ensemble to a Tchaikovsky string composition. The structure of *Serenade* foreshadowed all of the elements that would come to mark Balanchine's work: his favoritism of the female dancer, his disregard for acting or too much plot, his sharp simplicity, and, most of all, his musicality. It remains one of the most widely performed and popular of his works.

After several attempts to start a professional company as well as stints working in Hollywood and on Broadway, Balanchine finally founded the New York City Ballet (NYCB) in 1948 and with it began establishing his vision of what American neoclassical dance should be.

In 1934, George Balanchine founded the School of American Ballet; shortly thereafter he choreographed his first American ballet, *Serenade*, for his students. Here, the New York City Ballet performs *Serenade* at the New York State Theater at Lincoln Center.

THE WORLD ACCORDING TO MR. B

"Mr. B.," as his dancers affectionately called him, held strong opinions about dancing and dancers. First, he greatly preferred the female to the male dancer, insisting that women were the core and the soul of ballet. Men existed to showcase them. Women's bodies were naturally more flexible, and therefore their line was naturally more beautiful. As John Gruen recalled in the 1975 book *The Private World of Ballet*, Balanchine famously declared, "Ballet is a woman."

His views could at times seem obsessive. He preferred that his female dancers not marry, but he, in fact, married four ballerinas—Tamara Geva, Vera Zorina, Maria Tallchief, and Tanaquil Le Clercq—and lived with Alexandra Danilova. When his favorite dancer, Suzanne Farrell—with whom he was rumored to be in love—married fellow NYCB dancer Paul Mejia, Balanchine reportedly cut Mejia's roles, forcing the couple to leave the company. Still, in addition to Farrell, Balanchine's training produced some of the best dancers of the century in Merrill Ashley, Patricia McBride, Allegra Kent, and Kyra Nichols. His roster of great male students—Edward Villella, Jacques D'Amboise, and Peter Martins among them—proved that a dancer did not have to be his favorite in order to benefit from his tutelage.

As for physique, Balanchine preferred tall, long-limbed, long-necked dancers. He claimed there was more to see in a tall dancer—more line and extension. This preference, along with his Russian-bred technique, produced American dancing that was leaner, stronger, and crisper than any that had been seen before.

Balanchine also changed the historical role of the *corps de ballet*, negating the idea of a corps that exists only to perform ensembles as a backdrop for a soloist. His corps was the heart of his company from which his principal dancers were eventually singled out and nurtured. He also eschewed strict uniformity of movement in the corps and urged his corps dancers to express themselves individually. However, his corps pieces are among the most harmoniously danced works on the stage.

In addition to his theories on the corps, Balanchine deplored the "star system" of Europe in which companies courted and hosted touring guest artists to dance in front of their corps. Instead, Balanchine wanted each of his dancers to train hard and aspire to the rank of soloist. Although obviously not all of them would make it, the stars Balanchine did feature typically came out of his own corps in a "promote from within" system.

Perhaps Mr. B's biggest contribution is the storyless ballet. Although he staged some reproductions of romantic classics such as *Don Quixote*, he much preferred ballets without a narrative. "How much story do you want?" he said in the 1998 book *Ballet 101*. "You put a man and woman onstage together, and already it's a story." Instead of

SERENADE

Choreography by George Balanchine, 1934
Music by Pyotr Ilyich Tchaikovsky

The most popular and widely performed of Balanchine's ballets, *Serenade* was created as a training exercise for his students in the year after he opened the School of American Ballet. "I wanted to teach them how to be onstage," he said. It is widely considered the first plotless ballet and the beginning of Balanchine's brand of neoclassicism, showcasing his legendary musicality, symmetry, and speed. Danced in simple leotards and long tulle skirts, *Serenade* begins with the foundation of all classical ballet, a large corps of women moving in unison, and then mutates into various smaller combinations.

Balanchine imbued the ballet with the happenstances of real rehearsals—a woman falls to the floor and, exhausted, stays there; another enters late—and also with a contemplation on relationships between the sexes, as in a lovely, at times heartbreaking, dance between one man and three women. Starting with *Serenade*, Balanchine began

his choreography existing inside a fanciful narrative or fairy tale, it acts chiefly as a straightforward and simple showcase for virtuosic dancing set to orchestral music. For instance, *Agon* presents 12 dancers in practice clothes competing with each other. The *Four Temperaments* is simply a series of dances portraying one of the four medieval human temperaments—melancholic, sanguine, phlegmatic, and choleric—or, elementally speaking, earth, air, water, and fire.

Musicality is the last of Balanchine's hallmarks—connected, perhaps, to his early training as a pianist. Tying his steps closely to the score, his dances become almost balletic illustrations of the music, with the simple

his trademark of constructing dances that simultaneously test the caliber of a company while extracting from the music tremendous emotion in the simplest gestures—an arm moving slowly to the forehead, two dozen women in identical arabesque, a woman's hand placed just so on a man's shoulder. The result is both a standard and an artistic expression of the highest order.

If a company has a weak spot, Balanchine's choreography will reveal it. Is the corps moving with perfect timing? How many fast **piqués** (traveling moves up to *pointe*) can they do in a row? Can they all turn repeatedly without falling behind tempo? Balanchine's bias toward the female dancer is evident—only one man shows up onstage—and so is his belief in fostering a strong *corps de ballet* instead of exclusively nurturing only big names and principal dancers. In *Serenade*, as in subsequent works of Balanchine, all the traditional rules of ballet are intact, accounted for, and even improved upon. As a whole, his dancers routinely had better extension, strength, and line than those who came before them, but in his hands, those rules are stripped bare and made visible, with nothing extra coming between the dancer, the dance, and the audience.

scenery and costumes adding to the pared-down effect of a transparent vision of dance. The steps are not simply vehicles for expressing some imagined emotion but are the point of the piece and inherently contain the emotion themselves.

That is not to say that his ballets were not romantic or passionate; in fact, he believed that much of the passion of the dance came not from an overlaid story but from the intermingling of bodies themselves as they danced in groups, trios, and duos. Balanchine's dances can subtly imply an intensely romantic feeling, but this feeling arises naturally out of the choreography and not from a plot the audience reads in the program.

BALANCHINE TECHNIQUE

Balanchine's legacy is the result of much more than his preferences and personal philosophy. His precise, energetic, and musical approach was perfected day after day in class and in rehearsal, where his focus on the minutest details formed the basis of the "Balanchine technique" used in the School of American Ballet and the New York City Ballet to this day.

Balanchine's class technique was not theoretical, not a devotion to some pure blueprint of dance; it was directly related to the stage and to the audience's perception of the dancer. He knew an audience wanted to be captivated, hence his directive to dance "on top of the music," to move into the next step with great momentum and end each step on time, often with just a hint of a drawn-out flourish. He observed that the vertical line of the body is what gives a dance its sense of majesty and weightlessness, so he oriented his dancers on that line, insisting that the working leg move exactly perpendicular to the supporting one, that steps begin and end in a tightly closed fifth position (in which the back leg becomes nearly invisible), and that extensions to the front and back put the toe directly on the center line of the body.

His signature precision extended all the way down and up the dancer's body to the toes and fingers. He wanted the feet pointed not just through the arch, but all the way down to the tips of the toes, which for women meant curling the toes intensely to push the hard plaster of pointe shoes into a pleasing curve. Likewise, while most techniques favor a gracefully curved but not-too-evident hand, Balanchine wanted

Balanchine choreographed *Apollo* in 1928, and it has stood the test of time, as evidenced by this performance by Great Britain's Royal Ballet in 2007. Pictured here is Federico Bonelli in the role of Apollo.

all five fingers articulated. In a Balanchine hand, the thumb and middle finger curl in toward each other until they almost touch, and the pinky extends upward—seen from the front, the fingers separate much farther apart than in most other techniques, giving the impression of a flamenco dance.

Most of all, Balanchine demanded intensity and commitment to each movement—he berated dancers who approached a step without full energy, and this, in addition to his focus on the entire group as opposed to a few uniquely talented "stars," resulted in the sharp, quickened elegance that audiences expect in a Balanchine ballet. Of course, he wanted emotion too, and to feel a dancer's passion and individuality, but he wanted these aspects expressed through the language of perfect musicality and fully articulated line, and this is why audiences come in large numbers year after year to see New York City Ballet perform Balanchine masterpieces, such as *Allegro Brillante*, *Jewels*, and *Mozartiana*.

MINORITIES IN BALLET

Balanchine's less hierarchical, more "democratic" approach to running a company influenced, to a degree, his hiring decisions. In 1946, Balanchine married the world's first Native American prima ballerina, Maria Tallchief, a statuesque, strong, glorious soloist with the Ballets Russes de Monte Carlo. The following year, Tallchief joined the New York City Ballet, where Balanchine created various roles especially for her. Tallchief enraptured audiences with her lead role in Balanchine's version of *The Firebird*, and she was the NYCB's first-ever Sugarplum Fairy in his version of *The Nutcracker*.

Then, in 1955, Balanchine hired a 21-year-old named Arthur Mitchell, who became the first African American to dance with an American ballet company. Certainly this wasn't a complete surprise, given the increasing movement to support racial equality in the country at that time. But given ballet's aristocratic, European roots, and its public perception as a "high" and refined art, it is telling that Balanchine—who had left the rigid Soviet system to bask in the freedom and modernity of the West—brought Mitchell on and nurtured his career a full decade before the Civil Rights Voting Act was passed.

Mitchell shone at the NYCB, where he quickly rose to the position of principal dancer. In 1957, when Balanchine debuted *Agon*, he had created a *pas de deux* choreographed specifically for Mitchell and the ballerina Diana Adams, who was white. No one thought Balanchine did this for political reasons (Mr. B was concerned with art, not politics); nevertheless, the socially charged vision of a black man dancing so intimately and beautifully with a white woman drew both enthusiastic praise and angry protest. When *Agon* was shown on television, Southern television stations refused to air it; but Balanchine did not back down, refusing to recast the role with a white dancer for TV.

Mitchell performed at NYCB for 15 years and then, spurred by the death of Martin Luther King Jr., left to form his own company in Harlem, where he hoped to entice disadvantaged children to take interest in dance. Thus was born the Dance Theatre of Harlem, where Mitchell and his cofounder, Karel Shook, nurtured young African-American students and constructed a repertoire that showed the world a different face of classical ballet. In Mitchell's hands, *The Fire-*

bird was transformed from a feudal Russian fairy tale into a fantasy set in the Caribbean, and Giselle was not a heartbroken Austrian lass but the Creole mistress of a Louisiana plantation owner. Dance Theatre of Harlem did much to break down stereotypes and elitist perceptions of ballet and, on a more subtle level, helped pave the way for the combination of ballet and modern dance that emerged in the 1980s and 1990s.

NYCB VERSUS ABT

While Balanchine was developing his neoclassical, no-star company in New York City, dancer Lucia Chase had founded American Ballet Theatre (ABT, but originally known as just Ballet Theatre) in 1940, but a half-mile away. ABT was the United States' other great company, with a vision very different from Balanchine's. ABT focused equally on creating new ballets and restaging the great European classics such as *Giselle* and *La Bayadère* for American audiences. And instead of basing itself entirely in New York City, ABT became a touring company, taking its roster of Old World classics around the United States. Though it did eventually nurture its own generation of American dancers, it relied on touring European and Russian artists such as Alicia Markova, Anton Dolin, and Irina Baranova, who all came to ABT as guest artists over the years.

Between Balanchine's new brand of neoclassicism at New York City Ballet and Chase's popularizing of the classics at American Ballet Theatre, the United States in the 1960s began experiencing what ballet-watchers call a dance boom. It was kick-started in the 1950s, when America and the rest of the world got its first glimpse of Russia's two giants, the touring Kirov and Bolshoi ballets, which had been developing their ranks behind the Iron Curtain for three decades. Directly descended from the training of Petipa, Cecchetti, and Vaganova and funded generously from the beginning by the Soviet state, the Russians' technical virtuosity and dramatic scope greatly impressed international audiences. Russian dancers could leap higher and spin faster than any others in the world. One in particular, Rudolf Nureyev, became known unequivocally as the greatest male dancer of his generation.

NUREYEV, FONTEYN, AND THE DANCE BOOM

After defecting to France in 1961 (complete with a dramatic standoff between the KGB and French police at a Paris airport), Nureyev soon began working with the Royal Danish Ballet in Copenhagen and the Royal Ballet in London. Though he was 19 years younger than British prima ballerina Margot Fonteyn, de Valois saw in Fonteyn and Nureyev the makings of a legendary dance partnership. When approached, Fonteyn—then the most revered ballerina in the world—hesitated to partner with the young Russian nearly 20 years her junior. But she soon realized that Nureyev's appeal would captivate Western audiences and decided to take the risk of working with him instead of letting another ballerina get the chance.

Ninette de Valois's instinct was astute. Even before Fonteyn and Nureyev stepped onstage for their first performance together—the Royal Ballet's 1962 production of *Giselle* at London's Covent Garden—the public was clamoring for them. Seventy thousand ticket applications had to be turned down. Onstage, the duo surpassed everyone's expectations. The juxtaposition of the young Nureyev's fierce sensuality with Fonteyn's regal femininity made for brilliant chemistry, which the classical Romantic format showcased perfectly, sparking an immediate sensation. During the curtain call, when Fonteyn handed Nureyev a single rose from her bouquet and he knelt at her feet, the audience went wild.

The next year, the great choreographer Sir Frederick Ashton created a one-act ballet called *Marguerite and Armand* specifically for Fonteyn and Nureyev. Taken from the Alexandre Dumas (1824–1895) novel about a Parisian courtesan's self-sacrificing love affair with a younger man—the same novel that inspired Verdi's opera *La Traviata*—*Marguerite and Armand* became Fonteyn and Nureyev's signature work. Again, the duo affirmed the truism that opposites attract onstage: Nureyev's passionate athleticism played off Fonteyn's classic beauty and impeccable line like fire and ice. In her midst, the brilliant young dancer seemed to appear more gallant and refined; in his, the queenly Fonteyn softened, allowing a hint of sensuality to shimmer just below the surface of her performance. Their onstage chemistry, of course, and constant companionship while rehearsing and touring led many to believe the two were having an affair, though Fonteyn was married and Nureyev carried on numerous other relationships with both men and women. Although the question of an affair has never been settled, the verdict on their professional collaboration was never in doubt: Fonteyn and Nureyev, individually two of the best dancers of their time, created the most magical vision of Romantic ballet's masculine-feminine dynamic ever seen onstage. Their worldwide tours did as much to popularize ballet in the 1960s as Anna Pavlova's had earlier in the century.

In 1965, when they debuted Kenneth MacMillan's staging of the ultimate love story, *Romeo and Juliet*, Fonteyn was 46 (dancing the role of a 14-year-old). Ultimately, their partnership prolonged Fonteyn's career by more than a decade, as she danced well into her 50s—an unsurpassed achievement for a ballerina. The two remained lifelong friends, and Nureyev himself continued to draw crowds well into the 1980s, when he became artistic director of the Paris Opera Ballet. There, he nurtured several young dancers, including Sylvie Guillem, who went on to become one of the top ballerinas in the world. In 2000, seven years after Nureyev's death from AIDS, Guillem and Nicholas Le Riche performed in a revived staging of *Marguerite and Armand* at Covent Garden. Until then, no one other than Fonteyn and Nureyev had danced the roles, as Ashton had forbidden it—just one more way in which the legendary partnership of Fonteyn and Nureyev became immortalized in the hearts of balletomanes, as ardent admirers of the ballet are called.

THE MAGIC OF "MISHA"

If Balanchine brought classical ballet to the United States, and Nureyev grew its audience with his constant touring and virtuosic technique, a third Russian émigré cemented its vision in the eyes of Americans. Born in 1948, Mikhail Baryshnikov was 10 years younger than Nureyev and had studied at the Kirov's school with Nureyev's teacher, Alexander Pushkin. In 1974, while on tour with the Kirov Ballet in Canada, he defected and soon made his way to New York City.

Latvian-born dancer Mikhail Baryshnikov arrived in the United States in 1974, after first defecting from the Soviet Union to Canada. From 1974 to 1978, he was a principal dancer of the American Ballet Theatre. He is pictured performing as the Harlequin, with Patricia McBride as Columbine, in a performance of *Harlequinade* in January 1978.

At five feet seven inches tall, the young dancer was on the short side for a *premiere danseur*, yet in all other ways his physique was nearly perfect, an ideal vehicle to showcase his stunning technical ability and confident, masterful style. With large, muscular legs, Baryshnikov could leap high and land silently, appearing to glide through the air. His extension and point were superb as well, and he could turn repeatedly on a dime, landing cleanly right on top of the music. His performing strength lay in his ability to work his lower body so diligently, like an engine pushing a train, while his upper body, arms, and facial expression remained relaxed, confident, almost playful. In spite of his height, he also made for a strong partner, remaining in the background as he supported the woman and provided small flourishes of the feet and hands for her movements, but emerging as a virtuoso a few minutes later in his own solos and in the final codas of his *grand pas de deux*.

Baryshnikov landed in New York in 1974 and immediately signed on with American Ballet Theatre as a principal dancer. There, he worked with many choreographers, including Alvin Ailey and Twyla Tharp. In 1977, he also choreographed his own version of *The Nutcracker*, starring himself and Gelsey Kirkland, a petite and brilliant ballerina and a coalumnus of the Kirov with whom Baryshnikov was also romantically involved. This version was filmed for television and nominated for an Emmy Award. That same year, he was nominated for an Academy Award for his starring role in the film *The Turning Point*.

Though Baryshnikov's career was at its peak in 1978, he decided to put it all on hold and leave American Ballet Theatre in order to study with Balanchine at New York City Ballet, giving up a relatively large salary and star status in order to learn the American neoclassical style from the great teacher. Though Balanchine had refused to work with Nureyev and other Russian greats who had made their way to New York, he took "Misha" in, perhaps due to the young dancer's earnest willingness to humble himself in order to fit into Mr. B's nonstar system. "I felt I would kill myself if Mr. B didn't take me," Baryshnikov told *Time* magazine. "I realized I would never forgive myself if I did not try."

He spent only 15 months studying under Mr. B., but in that time, he learned 20 roles, appearing in Balanchine classics, such as *Apollo*, *Rubies*, and *Prodigal Son*. Then, in 1980, ABT offered Baryshnikov the position of artistic director upon Lucia Chase's retirement, and along with it the chance to execute his own artistic vision. He took the opportunity, with Mr. B's blessing, and continued to dance with ABT until 1985, becoming widely known to audiences through TV specials such as *Baryshnikov on Broadway* and *Baryshnikov in Hollywood*. The multitalented dancer was also nominated for a Tony Award for his role in Broadway's *Metamorphosis*.

From the 1990s until the present, Baryshnikov has focused on modern dance, founding the White Oak Project with modern choreographer Mark Morris in 1990 as a vehicle for older dancers, and in 2005, he started the Baryshnikov Arts Center in New York, where artists from various disciplines collaborate, create new work, and perform. As an actor, he also appeared in the TV series *Sex and the City*, as Carrie Bradshaw's lover Aleksandr Petrovsky, exposing him to an even wider (and younger) audience who had perhaps never seen him dance. Luckily, Baryshnikov's performances have been widely documented; dozens of DVDs capture him at his peak, giving future dance fans a glimpse of the man longtime *New York Times* dance critic Clive Barnes called "the most perfect dancer I have ever seen."

Thus, the nexus of the ballet world passed—with the help of three legendary Russian-born men—from Russia to the United States. By the second half of the twentieth century, America's ballet movement was in full swing with its own imported international stars, several large urban companies such as the San Francisco Ballet and the Boston Ballet, and its own uniquely American neoclassical vision. Balanchine himself summed it up when, upon arriving in Russia with the touring New York City Ballet in 1962, an interviewer said to him, "Welcome to Moscow, home of the classic dance."

"I beg your pardon," replied Mr. B, as recounted in *The Private World of Ballet*. "Russia is the home of the romantic ballet. The home of classic ballet is now America."

Ballet Goes Pop

In order to fully understand how ballet changed and became much more interesting and accessible to the general public in the late twentieth century, we first have to go back and look at modern dance and its progenitor, Isadora Duncan, at the turn of the twentieth century.

In a time when Petipa's traditional Romantic style still held sway over Europe and Russia, Duncan, a freethinking American with a love of music and ancient Greek culture, brought a completely new aesthetic to the stage. Declaring herself the enemy of ballet, whose structure she labeled superficial and elitist, she instead embraced a form of dance that was its opposite: natural, free, and unbounded by rules. She toured all over Europe and Russia, dancing alone, barefoot, and dressed in long, filmy tunics. The only traditional aspect of her performances was the music she chose—orchestral works by great composers such as Mendelssohn, Beethoven, and Chopin. Running, hopping, and improvising wildly with great freedom in her upper body, Duncan never failed to rouse audiences—a few hated her, but most loved her, and none could deny her authentic emotional expression.

Though Duncan died in 1927 after a tumultuous and often tragic life, others further developed her ideas. The first were Ruth St. Denis and Doris Humphrey, followed by Martha Graham, the doyenne of modern dance.

Graham not only eschewed ballet's turnout and historical positioning of the feet, as Duncan had earlier, but she completely invented her own style—angular, athletic, centered in the pelvis and low back, with a low center of gravity as opposed to ballet's airborne quality. Her dances expressed primal psychological states and the female psyche in particular. In fact, men did not appear in her company at all during its first decade—the 1930s. Still, even by then, modern dance was not so much ballet's enemy as a new branch on the tree of theatrical dance. Graham and other modernists insisted their dancers take ballet class as foundation training, which is still standard practice in modern dance companies.

Not only did modern dancers thus dabble in ballet, but soon ballet choreographers began incorporating into their work such modern techniques as parallel and flexed feet and sensual, almost acrobatic moves of the body against the floor. Even Balanchine collaborated with Graham in their jointly choreographed *Episodes* in 1959.

MODERN DANCE MINGLES WITH BALLET

One of the first classical choreographers to "loosen up" ballet was American-born Jerome Robbins, who studied modern, Spanish, and Oriental dance as well as ballet in his youth. Early in his career, which included many Broadway musicals and a stint as New York City Ballet's ballet master alongside Balanchine, he created his masterpiece for American Ballet Theatre. *Fancy Free*, which premiered during the height of World War II in 1944, featured three sailors on leave dancing to the music of Leonard Bernstein. Its combination of classical ballet steps and modern, jazzy Broadway moves marked Robbins's style for decades to come and was a sign of how modern and classical lines had blurred into what has been called "crossover ballet."

Another early creator of crossover ballets was Robert Joffrey, who also studied modern dance in addition to his ballet training at the School

Pictured here during a rehearsal for *Letter to the World* in 1945, choreographer/modern dancer Martha Graham revolutionized theatrical dance. Through her angular and athletic style, which emphasized a low center of gravity, she introduced primal psychological states and the female psyche into the genre.

of American Ballet. When Joffrey founded his own company in 1956, he focused on two things: restaging the classics of Nijinsky, Fokine, and others and commissioning modern dance choreographers to work with his company. He started the trend of ballet companies turning to modern choreographers for inspiration and variety.

One of Joffrey's commissions proved a pivotal point in the dialogue between ballet and modern dance. In 1973, dancer and choreographer Twyla Tharp—who had studied ballet with Antony Tudor and modern dance with Graham and others—made *Deuce Coupe* for Joffrey, set to the music of the Beach Boys. Three years later, American Ballet Theatre commissioned her work *Push Comes to Shove*, starring the inimitable Baryshnikov. Seeing the world's best male ballet dancer performing the relaxed, highly entertaining moves of Tharp gave the ballet world a populist jolt. It turned out that ballet dancers loved to work in the modern vein just as much as modern choreographers loved to fit their work onto

FANCY FREE

Choreography by Jerome Robbins, 1944
Music by Leonard Bernstein

In addition to being highly entertaining, *Fancy Free* is historically important as the first ballet created by Robbins, the first American-born ballet choreographer. For these reasons it has become known as a uniquely American masterwork. With only one act, which takes place on a summer night in New York City, and six characters—three sailors, two women, and a bartender—*Fancy Free* became an instant hit with audiences who needed a respite from World War II. Robbins mixed classical ballet moves with popular dances of the day while Bernstein's jazzy score blared in the background. Accessible and yet highly structured, the ballet was so popular it was expanded into a Broadway musical called *On the Town*, also choreographed by Robbins, and later into a film of the same name.

PUSH COMES TO SHOVE

Choreography by Twyla Tharp, 1976
Music by Joseph Lamb and Franz Joseph Haydn

If *Fancy Free* planted the seed of crossover ballet, *Push Comes to Shove* was crossover in full bloom 32 years later. Twyla Tharp, who had trained in both ballet and modern dance—the latter with Martha Graham and Graham disciple Paul Taylor—created a complete intermingling of classical ballet steps and modern dance for American Ballet Theatre. Alternating between the Rococo strains of Haydn's Symphony No. 82 and the ragtime piano of Joseph Lamb, *Push* features a male lead (originally Mikhail Baryshnikov, who helped make it a success), two female leads representing the two feminine ideals of classical ballet—the tall, elegant ballerina and the shorter, livelier one—and a small group of dancers who comprise a corps. Combining traditional leaps and *pirouettes* with slinky, loose steps and turns, and incorporating many heightened pauses when the dancers seem to ponder the music as well as their own dancing, *Push* surprises audiences. There are unexpected props such as a bowler hat and misplaced happenings such as a pair of dancers continuing on in silence after the music has ended or taking their bows in the middle of a dance. Though "abstract" and storyless, Tharp's choreography seems to ask questions about ballet itself, such as, "What if the man competes with the woman instead of lifting and supporting her?" and "Do the steps always have to be in sync with the music?" Tharp's sharp, witty moves create a thoughtful but also entertaining dance that ultimately leaves the audience filled with laughter as well as applause.

the well-trained and highly skilled bodies of ballet dancers, and audiences approved as well.

MODERN, OR CROSSOVER, BALLET

By the end of the 1970s, many a classical ballet company was incorporating modern steps into its repertoire and hiring modern choreographers to construct distinctive works on its own dancers, which the company would then fold into its repertoire of classics during a given season. But a few choreographers took the fusion of ballet and modern dance even further, creating dances that started to change the very definition of ballet.

One of the most acclaimed of these choreographers was Mark Morris, a dancer who had studied flamenco and folk styles before forming his own dance company in 1980. From the beginning, Morris defied convention, employing dancers of varying shapes, sizes, and ages and instilling an earthy naturalness in his dances, although they were highly structured and set to classical music. The outspoken Morris did not hesitate to inject humor into his work; yet his undeterred attention to detail, inventive choreography, and unfailing musicality balanced out his more edgy traits. Though his dancers performed barefoot and without turnout, his choreography displayed a delicate structure and intricacy; the result was a "balletic" type of modern dance not seen before.

His masterwork is 1988's *L'Allegro, Il Penseroso ed il Moderato*, a two-and-a-half-hour-long exploration of the "happy" and "contemplative" medieval temperaments, based on a Milton poem and set to a Baroque score by Handel. The juxtaposition of refined music, complex choreography, and inventive surprises (the women lift the men as well as vice versa) set the stage for a new kind of dance—at once earthbound and elegant—that blurred the boundaries between ballet and modern dance all the more. Morris continues to create new work not only for his Mark Morris Dance Group but for ballet companies worldwide, especially the San Francisco Ballet, for which he has created seven new works. His highly theatrical and humorous version of *The Nutcracker*, which he

Dancer, choreographer, and director Mark Morris is perhaps best known for his 1991 satirical version of *The Nutcracker*, called *The Hard Nut*, which takes place in a 1960s-era household. Here, at the end of the first act of *The Hard Nut* during a 2004 performance in London, dancers create a snowstorm.

titled *The Hard Nut*, brings the traditional German Christmas tale into a dysfunctional, 1960s-era household and, like many of his works, bends both gender roles and assumptions about classical ballet—as when he casts muscular men and women in flowing flower-petal skirts in a bare-foot, earthy "Waltz of the Flowers."

Another groundbreaking choreographer and contemporary of Morris who changed the way the world views ballet, William Forsythe only began studying ballet while in college. Though he eventually trained with both the Joffrey Ballet School and the School of American Ballet, it quickly became clear that Forsythe's natural gift lay in choreography. Soon after joining the Stuttgart Ballet in 1973, he became its choreographer-in-residence at the young age of 27, and by 1984 Forsythe had been named ballet director of the Frankfurt Ballet, where he remained for 20 years, creating dozens of seminal works that examined, critiqued, and ultimately redefined the ballet. His breakthrough work, 1987's *In the Middle, Somewhat Elevated*, an abstract piece for four dancers set to the percussive electronic music of Thom Willem, showcases the physical beauty of ballet—its sky-high extensions and multiple *pirouettes*—but in a forceful way. In its *pas de deux*, the dancers twist around each other in a push-pull that is sometimes lyrical and almost snakelike, sometimes angular as if they were struggling against one another. The following year, Forsythe folded *In the Middle* into a three-act work called *Impressing the Czar*—the name of which directly critiques the goal of nineteenth-century Russian romantic ballet: not necessarily to express human art and feeling in the deepest way, but to impress the aristocracy. In it, Forsythe injects fragments from ballet's past—from its court costumes and poses to its neoclassical precision and technicality—into a cacophonous medley of dance and dance commentary that includes singing, speaking, and even rap. In the final act, when 40 women and men dressed in schoolgirl uniforms stomp rebelliously in a circle around a languishing figure of a saint shot through with arrows, the implication is clear: The restrictions classical ballet has imposed on human movement will, ultimately, never be as lasting or as significant as the primal will to dance. And yet, by inserting the classically brilliant and virtuosic *In the Middle* within *Impressing the Czar*, Forsythe simultaneously preserves the barebones beauty of the balletic form, pointing out both its sublimity and its flaws all at once.

A NEW DEFINITION

Thanks to choreographers such as Morris, Forsythe, and a host of others who deconstructed and added to the balletic lexicon, today's ballet-goer has the widest possible array of choices. Nearly every U.S. city has its own professional company that performs both Romantic classics and American neoclassical and modern crossover ballets, and both national and international troupes tour widely. Today's balletgoers can see the Joffrey Ballet perform its restaging of Nijinsky's infamous *Le Sacre du Printemps* or its 1992 ballet *Billboards*, set to the music of Prince. He or she can see the classical *Swan Lake* or opt for Matthew Bourne's version featuring a male "swan queen" and a cast of all-male swans: barefoot, muscular, and faces painted with ominous black beaks.

William Forsythe's three-act ballet *Impressing the Czar* is a satire about Western civilization from the Renaissance to modern times. Here, Geneviève Van Quaquebeke and Sanny Kleef of the Royal Ballet perform the ballet at Sadler's Wells Theater in London.

With all this crossover going on, how do we define ballet as it exists right now? In strictly traditional terms, ballet must adhere to the rules of the danse d'école established in France in the seventeenth century. Some of those conventions include turnout, the defined vocabulary of steps such as *jetés* and *arabesques*, pointed feet, ballet line, and women dancing *en pointe*. These days, most choreographers take the artistic liberty of bending those rules, creating all kinds of interesting and lasting combinations of movement. As long as the choreographer and the dancers work from the rules as a foundation—even if bending and reworking them—the work is often classified as ballet.

At its core, though, ballet is not merely about rules. The rules exist only to serve its real purpose: to present the human body at its height of strength, beauty, and grace—qualities that dancers and choreographers

In 1995, British choreographer Matthew Bourne introduced his version of *Swan Lake*, which features an all-male corps and two male leads. Here, dancers perform Bourne's version of *Swan Lake* in Melbourne, Australia, in April 2007. Bourne won three Tony Awards for his Broadway production of the classic.

train for decades to develop using the language of turnout, extension, and line.

There is something else, however, at the heart of ballet. Its emotional center is sensual and romantic—some would say even sexual. If a performance is a classic in the vein of Petipa's works, the old-fashioned notion of chivalry no doubt plays a huge part in both the storyline and the dancing itself—the strong man supporting and protecting the woman, and the woman displaying an ethereal feminine grace. In more modern fare, there are fewer gender roles at play, but they are replaced with a raw bodily energy that is more honest and natural. From any viewpoint, ballet is about the body—the bodies of men and women, either in an ideal form similar to a moving sculpture or in more natural and vulnerable form. The bodies are always beautiful and, like all art, their movements create emotion—and sometimes new ways of looking at the world.

Now that ballet is "out of the box" of its strictly classical structure, it is bound to spread in even more imaginative directions. Though the great classics continue to thrive, one can assume that dancemakers will bend even more rules. This does not mean, however, that at some point in the future, toe shoes and the five positions will be retired.

A world without dancers performing *Swan Lake* would be akin to a world without actors doing *Hamlet* or a world without musicians playing Beethoven. Though it may expand far afield of its origins, as long as music inspires and physical strength and beauty enthrall people, ballet is bound to survive—carrying forward both its Old World traditions and charms as well as its modern bursts of imagination.

A Basic
Ballet Class

So what does ballet look like? What is it actually composed of? All the mechanics of ballet are evident in a typical class, the structure of which is consistent throughout the world, regardless of country, teacher, or even the particular school of ballet being taught.

At any large ballet school, and even at most smaller regional schools meant to train nonprofessionals, the ballet class is accompanied by live piano. In some instances, the teacher will use a recorded album of piano accompaniment, but the presence of a pianist serves two important aims: It keeps up a spontaneous, noninterrupted flow of accompaniment to the dancers' work—for often the teacher will stop mid-exercise to illustrate or correct, or want to change the tempo—and it trains the dancer on a daily basis to work in sync with live classical music.

THE BARRE

Ballet class begins at the *barre*—a thin wooden pole running parallel to the walls of the room and horizontally, a little above waist level. With the support of the barre, dancers work one side of the body at a time, first

A seven-year-old boy leaps in the air for a teacher during May 2009 auditions for the American School of Ballet at the Lincoln Center in New York. The School of American Ballet is the official school of the New York City Ballet and begins accepting students at the age of six.

holding on with the left hand and working the right leg (in which case the right is called "the working leg," while the left is "the supporting leg"), then turning and holding on with the right hand to work the left leg. When considering the strain of 180-degree turnout and how long it takes to train the lower body into this mold while maintaining balance, the importance of the barre becomes evident. (Try it. Turn your feet all the way out so that the toes point away from each other in a straight line. Chances are you will begin to lose your balance, even more so if you try to move one foot anywhere while keeping the supporting leg turned out.)

Barre exercises begin with *plié*, the bending of the knees to warm up the leg muscles. *Pliés* are done in first, second, **third**, **fourth**, and

fifth positions. A bend while keeping the heels on the floor is called *demi-plié*; a full deep bend allowing the heels to lift is **grand plié**.

Dancers then proceed to **tendu** (or *battement tendu*), in which the working leg pushes out from **first position** until the heel lifts off the floor into an arched point to the front, side, and back. Though they look like small, simple movements, tendus develop the beginning of a dancer's point, extension, and line, training the legs to move out from and back into the two most important positions of the feet—first and fifth—while keeping the rest of the body tall, centered, and stationary. Thus, teachers spend a great deal of time on them.

Battement tendu then proceeds to *battement dégagé*, which looks similar except the leg is brushed slightly off the floor, and to *grand battement*, in which the leg extends far up into the air.

Barre work also includes *retiré*, in which the working leg is bent and lifted so that the pointed toe touches the inner knee of the supporting leg (later this position will be used for pirouettes); **port de bras**, or "carriage of the arms," in which the working arm moves through its own five positions; and **grand port de bras**, during which the dancer bends the upper body all the way forward to the floor and then all the way up into a deep backbend while working the arms. The positioning of the arms, the exact curve of the elbow and wrist, and especially the placement of each finger are matters of debate among the different ballet schools and their various teachers.

This is another instance of the great importance placed on the visual line, in which the arms and hands play such a vital role. In general, the arms are softly curved from a relaxed shoulder and rounded elbow with the wrist higher than the fingers. The fingers gently curve and extend so that the very tip of the dancer's line does not end abruptly but seems to trace off into the air around him or her. The thumb is generally held a few inches from the other fingers, the middle finger curves in the most, and the pinky and index fingers curve the least.

It may seem picky, but even a first-time balletgoer would be sure to notice a dancer whose arms and hands are held stiffly or straight instead of curving in this way. Indeed, the goal of *port de bras* is to convey an always graceful, relaxed, and flowing carriage of the arms, no matter how difficult the step that the lower body is attempting. A dancer may be performing a giant leap or several *pirouettes*, or trying with all her might to balance for several seconds on the tiptoes of one foot, but her upper body must never betray her effort. It must look relaxed, tall, and confident as the athleticism unfolds below. This holds true for the neck, head, eyes, and face as well, which are often slightly angled away from the direction of the lower body's movement in order to offset the visual line, adding a touch of panache to the step.

At some point in barre work, the dancer will begin to lift either the supporting foot or both feet into *relevé*, in which the heel lifts high off the floor and the foot arches. In the case of men and women who are not yet working *en pointe*, the body balances high on the ball of the foot. In the case of women dancers taking classes in their pointe shoes, *relevé* proceeds all the way up to *pointe* so that the entire foot is arched. If the curve of the arm and hand illustrate the top of the dancer's line, the foot in *relevé* is the basis for the bottom of it—and a perfectly arched foot balanced inside a long satin toe shoe produces quite a stunning visual effect.

ADAGIO

As the dancers leave the support of the barre and move into **center exercises**, or "floor work," the difficulty increases. Their sole support and balance must now come from a strong center, which emanates from straight legs in a tight fifth position; pulled-in abdominal muscles and a tucked-under pelvis so that there is no arch in the back (forming as straight a line as possible); and a lifted chest and head. Even when standing still, a dancer should feel that an invisible cord is running up through his or her body and out of her head, pulling him or her toward the ceiling.

Floor work begins with *adagio*—slow, graceful steps that focus on balance, line, extension, and control. In ***développés***, the pointed toe of the working leg traces its way up the supporting leg, extends high to either the front, side, or back, and then is held in the extended position—much like a kick in very slow motion. More than any other step, *développés* show a dancer's extension, or how high he or she can lift and hold an extended leg away from his or her body while keeping proper form (hips and shoulders squared). Though audiences may not know the technical name, good extension is quite easy to appreciate even for a

Ballerinas practice adagio—slow, graceful steps—during rehearsal. *Adagio* (*arabesque, shown above*) is used as a tool to strengthen a dancer's ability to control his or her balance and enhance extension.

first-time balletgoer. High extensions in **second position**—straight out to the side—are especially difficult and impressive. Most people have seen a photo of a ballerina with a straight leg extended up toward her ear.

Adagio inevitably includes *arabesques* and their counterpart, attitudes. In *arabesque*, the leg is lifted straight behind the torso, with the arms usually moving through various positions. A dancer's line can perhaps best be seen in his or her *arabesque*. Both the supporting leg—whether flat on the floor or *en pointe*—and the working leg are turned out, while the working hip is lifted only enough to allow the leg to reach higher, the shoulders are square, the arms are curved and soft, and the chin is lifted. Finally, the lifted foot is completely pointed, preferably with the toe angled higher than the heel. All these details can seem mundane, but remember that ballet's goal is to trace beautiful angles, curves, and patterns with the body. The difference between an arabesque that does not employ them and one that does is quite obvious to the eye; the former will look clumsy and stilted, the latter symmetrical and uplifted.

Attitude (the position invented by Carlo Blasis) is much like *arabesque* except that the lifted leg is bent at the knee instead of straight. Unlike *arabesque*, attitude can also be performed in front of the body or to the side, not only in back.

ALLEGRO

The *adagio* portion of the class gives way to *allegro*, a faster, livelier set of steps that focus on turning and leaping. *Jetés*, which translate simply as "thrown," are the groundwork for much of *allegro*. They are leaps from one foot to the other and can be done in any direction. They can be small and almost unnoticeable onstage or take the form of *grand jeté*, the huge running leap dancers take that frequently features a midair split. *Grand jeté en tournant* is a large jeté performed while the dancer spins her body in the air.

Pirouettes, turns on one leg with the other lifted usually toe to knee (though the lifted leg can also be extended in attitude or often second position), are practiced during *adagio* too. Pirouettes are an art and science all to themselves and take many years to master. Multiple *pirouettes* are even more difficult, and are definitely one of the steps an audience looks for in a performance. The most virtuosic form of pirouettes are *fouettés*, in which the working leg does not touch the ground between turns but whips out to the side before pulling in for the next rotation. Both *Swan Lake* and *Don Quixote* feature scenes in which the lead ballerina performs 32 *fouettés* uninterrupted, usually finishing off the last one with a multiple pirouette for flourish to loud applause.

Unlike pirouettes, which originate from the standing leg simply by lifting the working leg, *piqué* turns involve the dancer throwing a leg out and then turning onto it. When a ballerina completes a solo performing fast turns with one leg bent to the knee while moving in a large circular pattern around the stage, she is doing *piqués*. *Piqué* is a step in and of itself and consists simply of moving in any direction from *plié* onto one straight leg in *relevé*; it is the main way dancers move themselves about the stage.

A ballerina performs a *pirouette* during a rehearsal. This photo shows the strength and agility it takes to turn on one leg while the other is being lifted toe to knee.

Piqué turns often give way to ***chaînés***, a series of very fast turns in which the legs are kept close together and the weight moves quickly and almost imperceptibly from foot to foot. When a dancer finishes off a solo with spins that look like he or she is twirling on ice or unwinding like a spool of thread, he or she is performing chaînés.

Entrechats are another virtuosic step, performed mainly by male dancers. They begin in fifth position *plié* from which the dancer jumps straight into the air, beating his feet in a quick "exchange" front to back as many times as possible before landing. In *entrechat dix*, the maximum achieved so far, the legs cross six times in the air.

Tour en l'airs, another specialty of the men, involve leaving the floor from *plié* into a high, straight spin of the body, ending in plié. Both tours and entrechats show a dancer's strength and elevation, or what is often called his "attack," and multiple tours can be quite breathtaking to witness onstage.

Ballet class ends with reverence—traditional bows (for the men) or low curtsies (for the women) to the teacher. This is not a quick thank-you but a long, slow bending to the ballet master, steeped in decorum and performed to music, which also gives the dancers practice for graceful bowing onstage.

CHRONOLOGY

1489 A fete in Tortona, Italy, includes music, recitation, and self-contained dances called *entrées*.

1494 France's Charles II invades Naples and discovers Italian court dances called *balli*.

1533 Catherine de Medici marries Henry II of France, introducing Italian *balli* to the French court.

1581 *Le Ballet Comique de la Reine*, the first court ballet, is staged by the de Medici's for a relative's wedding.

1584 Teatro Olimpico in Vicenza, Italy, opens with a proscenium arch stage.

1605 Masques (English court ballets, performed along with poetry readings, music, and fireworks) begin to appear in London.

1651 King Louis XIV appears as Apollo in *Le Ballet de la Nuit*.

1661 Louis XIV creates the Académie Royale de Danse.

1669 Louis XIV creates Académie Royale de la Musique (Paris Ópera), run by Jean-Baptiste Lully. Ballet moves from the palace ballroom to a proscenium arch theater.

1681   The first professional female dancer, Madamoiselle Lafontaine, appears in *Le Triomphe de l'Amour* in Paris.

1726   Marie-Anne de Cupis de Camargo makes her debut in Paris.

1727   Marie Sallé makes her debut in Paris.

1738   Empress Anna Ivanovna founds Imperial Ballet School in St. Petersburg, Russia, directed by Jean-Baptise Landé.

1758   Jean Georges-Noverre begins producing *ballets d'action*.

1760   Noverre publishes his *Letters on Dancing and Ballets*.

1781   Noverre is appointed ballet master at King's Theatre in London.

1789   Jean Dauberval's *La Fille Mal Gardée* premieres in Bordeaux, France.

        The French Revolution commences.

1796   Charles-Louis Didelot produces *Flora and Zephyr* in London, which introduced dancing from wires, or "flying ballet."

1813   Imperiale Regia Accademia di Danze is established at La Scala in Milan.

1820   Carlo Blasis writes *An Elementary Treatise upon the Theory and Practice of the Art of Dancing*.

1825   Moscow's Bolshoi Theatre opens.

1830   Blasis publishes *The Code of Terpsichore*.

1832   Marie Taglioni dances *en pointe* in *La Sylphide* in Paris.

1834   Fanny Elssler debuts at Paris Opera.

1837	Blasis appointed director of La Scala's dance academy.
1841	*Giselle*, by Jean Coralli and Jules Perrot, premieres in Paris starring Carlotta Grisi.
1869	Marius Petipa's *Don Quixote* premieres in Moscow.
1870	Petipa is named grand ballet master at the Imperial Russian Ballet in St. Petersburg.
1877	Petipa's *La Bayadere* premieres in St. Petersburg.
1890	Petipa's *The Sleeping Beauty* premieres in St. Petersburg; Enrico Cecchetti becomes dancer and ballet master at the Imperial Russian Ballet, along with Petipa.
1892	Petipa's *The Nutcracker* premieres in St. Petersburg.
1895	Petipa and Lev Ivanov premiere a revival of the 1877 ballet *Swan Lake* in St. Petersburg.
1905	Pavlova performs Michael Fokine's *The Dying Swan* in St. Petersburg.
1909	Serge Diaghilev present Ballets Russes' first season in Paris.
1910	Chicago Opera Ballet is established.
1912	Vaslav Nijinsky debuts *L'après-midi d'un Faune* for Ballets Russes.
1917	The Russian Revolution takes place; Agrippina Vaganova begins teaching at the Maryinsky (aka Kirov) Ballet.
1924	George Balanchine joins Ballets Russes.
1931	Ninette de Valois becomes director of the Vic-Wells Ballet (later renamed Sadler's Wells Ballet in 1935 and Royal Ballet in 1956).

1933 San Francisco Ballet is founded by Adolph Bolm.

1934 Balanchine and Lincoln Kirstein found School of American Ballet; Margot Fonteyn debuts with the Vic-Wells Ballet in London; Vaganova publishes *Basic Principles of Classical Ballet.*

1935 Balanchine premieres *Serenade* in New York.

1940 Lucia Chase and Richard Pleasant found the Ballet Theatre in New York; it becomes the American Ballet Theatre in 1957.

1944 Jerome Robbins premieres *Fancy Free* in New York.

1948 The New York City Ballet is born.

1956 The Joffrey Ballet is established.

1959 The Bolshoi Ballet makes its first appearance in New York.

1957 Balanchine's *Agon* premieres in New York.

1961 Kirov Ballet begins touring the West.

1962 Rudoff Nureyev joins Royal Ballet and begins partnership with Fonteyn.

1963 Virginia Williams founds Boston Ballet.

1965 Balanchine's *Don Quixote* premieres in New York; Fonteyn and Nureyev appear in Kenneth Macmillan's *Romeo and Juliet* in London.

1967 Balanchine's *Jewels* premieres in New York.

1971 Dance Theatre of Harlem gives its first performance.

1974 Mikhail Baryshnikov defects to the West.

1976 Twyla Tharp choreographs *Push Comes to Shove*, considered one of the first crossover ballets, for the American Ballet Theatre.

1980 Baryshnikov becomes artistic director of the American Ballet Theatre.

Mark Morris establishes the Mark Morris Dance Group in New York City.

1983 Balanchine dies, leaving Peter Martins and Jerome Robbins as co-ballet masters in chief of the New York City Ballet; Nureyev becomes artistic director of the Paris Opera Ballet.

1984 Choreographer William Forsythe becomes ballet director at the Frankfurt Ballet.

1987 The George Balanchine Trust is established to protect and preserve Balanchine's works as he intended them.

1990 Baryshnikov and Morris form the White Oak Dance Project to showcase experienced dancers who had aged beyond ballet's traditional age limit.

1991 Morris choreographs *The Hard Nut*, his satirical pop-culture take on *The Nutcracker*; it premieres on national television (PBS) in 1992.

1993 Nureyev dies.

1995 London's Royal Ballet premieres Matthew Bourne's gender-bending *Swan Lake,* featuring an all-male corps and two male leads.

2000 Suzanne Farrell, known as Balanchine's last "muse," founds the Suzanne Farrell Ballet.

2003 Sylvie Guillem and Jonathan Cope star in the Royal Ballet's *Marguerite and Armand*, the first time the ballet is danced without Fonteyn and Nureyev, for whom it was choreographed.

2005 Baryshnikov creates the Baryshnikov Arts Center in New York, where artists from various disciplines collaborate, create new work, and perform.

2008   Influential dance critic Clive Barnes dies. Alexei Ratmansky steps down as artistic director of the Bolshoi Ballet to eventually choreograph at the American Ballet Theatre, among others.

2009   The Royal Ballet performs in Cuba; it is the first major ballet company to perform there since the Bolshoi did so about 30 years ago.

GLOSSARY

Adagio (*uh-dah-zheo*)   Slow and sustained movements performed during the second part of a ballet class and focused on balance and control; a slow and sustained dance in a ballet

Allegro *(uh-leh-gro)*   Fast running and jumping movements performed during the last part of a ballet class; a fast, lively dance in a ballet

Arabesque (*ara-besk*)   A common position in which the weight of the body is supported on one leg while the other is extended in back, leg straight. The arabesque may be varied in many ways by changing the position of the arms, the angle of the body, and the height of the leg in the air.

Attitude   A classical position similar to the *arabesque*, except the knee of the raised leg is bent

Balancé (*ba-lohn-say*)   A waltz step. On a count of 1-2-3, the working leg steps to the side in plié (1), the supporting leg follows behind, stepping onto the ball of the foot (2), and then the weight is transferred to the working leg again (3). Balancés can also be done to the front and back or turning.

Ballet masters   An old-fashioned term that basically means "choreographers"

Ballon (ba-lahn)   The appearance of weightlessness and of being airborne. A dancer is said to have ballon if he seems to be in the air constantly with only momentary contact with the floor.

Barre (*bar*)   A long wooden pole horizontally attached to the walls of a dance studio upon which dancers traditionally do warm-up exercises

Battement (*baht-mahn*)   An extension of the leg. Some variations are *grand battement* and *petit battement*.

Battement tendu (*baht-matin tahn-du*)   An exercise in which the working foot slides out from either first or fifth position to a pointed toe, never leaving the floor. Critical for learning to move the foot quickly and gracefully while maintaining placement, Balanchine considered it the most important exercise in all of ballet. Also simply called *tendu*.

Bourée (*boo-ray*)   A rapid traveling step, like a trill on the points of the toes, with the feet in fifth position. The feet move so quickly that the transfer of weight is almost imperceptible and the ballerina seems to skim across the stage.

Center exercises   Exercises done freely in the center of the room, as opposed to those done with the support of the barre

Chainé (*sheh-nay*)   A series of turns, executed in a line or in a circle, in which the feet remain together and the weight is transferred rapidly and almost imperceptibly from one foot to the other as the body revolves

Chassé (*shah-say*)   A slide in which the weight is transferred from two feet to one, or from one to another

Choreographer   The person who creates, or composes, dance

Coda   The final section of a *pas de deux*, in which the partners reunite to fast, lively music

Corps de ballet (*cor-du-ba-ley*)   The supporting dancers of the ballet company, whose role is often to perform group dances in unison

Danseur (*dan-sir*)   A professional male dancer

Développé (*deh-vel-oh-pay*)   A smooth, gradual unfolding of the leg toward the front, side, or back. The working leg is drawn up to the knee of the supporting leg and from there smoothly out to a position in the air, usually at 90 degrees or higher.

Divertissement (*dee-vert-tis-mahn*)   Meaning "diversion," a typically short dance in a classical ballet that has little to do with the plot but provides variety for the audience. Examples of divertissements are the themed dances in Act II of *The Nutcracker* and Act III of *Swan Lake*.

Elevation   The ability to jump high in the air. A step of elevation is a jump.

En l'air (*ahn lair*)   Used to describe movements in which the working leg is raised a considerable distance off the ground

En pointe (*ahn point*)   On the tips of the toes. Originally dancers did this in soft slippers; today toe shoes are blocked across the toe section to give added support.

Entrechat (ahn-treh-shah)   A jump beginning and ending in fifth position. While the body is in the air, the feet are rapidly crossed two or more times.

Extension   The ability to raise the working leg high in the air. Good extension comes from a combination of inborn flexibility and training.

Fifth Position   With both feet touching, the toes of each foot reach the heel of the other foot.

First Position   The balls of the feet are turned out completely. The heels touch each other and the feet face outward, trying to form a straight line.

Fouetté (*fweh-tay*)   One of the most brilliant steps in ballet. The dancer repeatedly turns on one foot (usually *en pointe*) as in *pirouette*, but between each revolution the working leg whips sharply into second position *en l'air* (in the air).

Fourth Position   The feet are placed the same as third position, but one step apart.

French School   The school of classical ballet known for its elegance and grace as opposed to technical strength and virtuosity

Glissade (*glih-sahd*)   A sliding step, beginning and ending in fifth position, usually done to the side

Grand battement (*grahn baht-mahn*)   A "kick" in which the working leg is raised as high as possible while keeping the rest of the body still. The movement is controlled as the leg lifts and as it comes down; the leg cannot be thrown.

Grand jeté (*grahn zheh-tay*)   A long horizontal jump, usually forward, starting from one leg and landing on the other. In the middle of the jump, the dancer may be doing a split in midair. One of the most memorable of all ballet jumps; the dancer seems to float in the air.

Grand pas de deux (*grahn pah deh duh*)   See *pas de deux*

Italian School   The school of ballet known for its high jumps, multiple turns, and athletic strength. Its master teacher was Enrico Cecchetti.

Jeté (*zheh-tay*)   A jump from one foot to the other foot, throwing the working leg out and then landing on it. The most common variation is a *grand jeté*.

Line   The harmonious alignment of the various parts of the dancer's body, the visual trace of which extends outward from the limbs in every direction, beyond them

Pas de chat (pah deh shah)   Literally translates as "leap of the cat," a *pas de chat* is a fast jump in which first one leg, then the other quickly leaves the ground with the knee bent, giving the effect of the legs forming a diamond shape in midair. In the famous "Dance of the Cygnets" in *Swan Lake*, the four cygnets perform 16 *pas de chat*.

Pas de deux (*pah deh duh*)   Literally "step for two," a duet, often in several sections, beginning with a partnered adagio, followed by the man's allegro, the woman's allegro, and finally the coda. Sometimes called a *grand pas de deux*.

Piqué (*pee-kay*)   A step up onto one foot with the other foot lifted to the knee or in the air

Pirouette (*pir-roh-wet*)   A turn in place, on one foot. A good dancer can execute four or five continuous revolutions; a virtuoso, as many as a dozen. During multiple pirouettes, the dancer uses spotting to avoid becoming disoriented. Pirouettes are usually fast, but supported pirouettes, in which a partner steadies the soloist at the waist or by a hand above the head, may be done very slowly.

Plié (*plee-ay*)   A bend of the knees, normally the first exercise done in ballet class. *Demi-plié* is a small bend with the heels on the floor; *grand plié* is a deep bend to where the thighs are nearly horizontal.

Pointe   See *en pointe*

Pointe shoes   See *toe shoes*

Port de bras (*por-deh-brah*)   The carriage of the arms. In *grand port de bras*, the dancer also moves the torso along with the arms, bending all the way down to the floor, then back up and then backward in a slight backbend.

Prima ballerina   The principal female dancer in a ballet company

Relevé (*re-leh-vay*)   A movement in which the heels are raised off the floor. The rise may be smooth or aided by a slight spring. If wearing soft shoes, the dancer balances on the ball of the foot. If wearing pointe shoes, she balances on the tip of the toes.

Retiré (*reh-teer-ay*)   A position in which the working foot is drawn up to the knee of the supporting leg

Russian School   The school of classical ballet that combined elements of French gracefulness and Italian athleticism. Its methods of instruction were perfected and documented by Agrippina Vaganova with the Vaganova system.

Second Position   The balls of both feet are turned out completely, with the heels separated by the length of one foot. Similar to first position, but the feet are spread apart.

Spotting   A technique for keeping oriented and avoiding dizziness during turns. The dancer picks a spot and keeps his or her eyes focused on it even as the body begins to turn. When the head finally follows the body into the turn, he or she quickly whips it around to find the spot again.

Technique   The detailed craft of dancing, built through repetition of exercises. A dancer with good technique displays proper skill in turnout, elevation, extension, line, upper body carriage, strength, and endurance.

Tendu (*tahn-du*)   Short for *battement tendu*

Terre à terre (*tair ah tair*)   Used to describe steps in which the dancer's feet do not leave the floor, or barely leave the floor

Third Position   One foot is in front of the other with the heel of the front foot touching the middle of the back foot.

Toe shoes   Soft fabric (usually satin) slippers blocked across the toes with extra material and hard glue to give support when the dancer rises *en pointe*

Tour en l'air (*tour ahn le-air*)   A complete single, double, or triple turn in the air, usually beginning from and ending in fifth position. It is almost always executed by male dancers.

Turnout   The balletic stance in which the legs are rotated outward so that the legs (and feet) point in opposite directions, ideally in a straight line. Turnout must begin at the hip. Forcing the feet and letting the knees, legs, and hips follow puts severe strain on the joints.

Tutu The traditional ballet skirt, usually made of many layers of gathered tulle. The length of the tutu varies according to the period or style of the ballet being performed.

Vaganova system A detailed system of instruction developed by Agrippina Vaganova to develop dancers of the Russian School

Virtuoso Though in general meaning simply having great skill, in classical ballet a virtuoso usually refers to a dancer with supreme athletic skill in particular—able to turn fast, leap high, and balance for long periods—as opposed to skills of grace or presentation (though virtuosos may also possess those).

BIBLIOGRAPHY

Acocella, Joan, ed. *The Diary of Vaslav Nijinsky*. New York: Farrar, Straus and Giroux, 1999.

Boorstin, Daniel. *The Creators: A History of the Heroes of the Imagination*. New York: Vintage Books, 1992.

Clarke, Mark, and Clement Crisp. *Ballet: An Illustrated History*. New York: Universe Books, 1973.

Craine, Debra, and Judith Mackrell. *The Oxford Dictionary of Dance*. New York: Oxford University Press, 2000.

Greskovic, Robert. *Ballet 101: A Complete Guide to Learning and Loving the Ballet*. New York: Hyperion, 1998.

Gruen, John. *The Private World of Ballet*. New York: Viking Press, 1975.

Ryman, Rhonda. *Dictionary of Classical Ballet Terminology*. Hightstown, N.J.: Princeton Book Company, 1997.

Schorer, Suki. *Suki Schorer on Balanchine Technique*. New York: Knopf, 1999.

Steeh, Judith. *History of Ballet and Modern Dance*. New York: Galahad Books, 1982.

Taper, Bernard. *Balanchine: A Biography*. Berkeley: University of California Press, 1984.

FURTHER RESOURCES

PUBLICATIONS

Acocella, Joan, ed. *Baryshnikov in Black and White*. New York: Bloomsbury USA, 2002.

Barber, David W. *Tutus, Tights and Tiptoes: Ballet History as It Ought to Be Taught*. Toronto: Sound & Vision Limited, 2000.

Dance Magazine, 111 Myrtle St., Suite 203, Oakland, Calif. 94607, 510-839-6060 or available online at *www.dancemagazine.com*.

Ellison, Nancy, and American Ballet Theatre. *The Ballet Book: Learning and Appreciating the Secrets of Dance*. New York: Universe Publishing, 2003.

Gottlieb, Robert. *George Balanchine: The Ballet Maker*. New York: Harper Collins, 2004.

Hammond, Sandra Noll. *Ballet Basics* (fourth edition). New York: McGraw-Hill, 1999.

Kavanagh, Julie. *Nureyev: The Life*. New York: Pantheon, 2008.

Kirkland, Gelsey. *Dancing on My Grave: An Autobiography*. New York: Berkeley Publishing Group, 1996.

Minden, Eliza Gaynor. *The Ballet Companion: A Dancer's Guide to the Technique, Traditions, and Joys of Ballet*. New York: Simon & Schuster, 2005.

Ramsey, Christopher, ed. *Tributes: Celebrating Fifty Years of the New York City Ballet*. New York: William Morrow, 1998.

Thalia, Mara. *The Language of Ballet: A Dictionary*. Hightstown, N.J.: Princeton Book Company, 1988.

WEB SITES

American Ballet Theatre

www.abt.org

This is the official Web site of the American Ballet Theatre, America's national ballet company.

Andros on Ballet

http://androsdance.tripod.com/home.html

Ballet teacher and writer Dick Andros provides a collection of articles about ballet history and classical ballet technique.

Ballet Alert

www.balletalert.com

This site offers the archives of the newsletter *Ballet Alert*, along with links and information on companies and dancers.

The Royal Ballet

www.roh.org.uk

This is the official site of England's Royal Ballet, the internationally renowned classical ballet company.

The History of Ballet

www.ccs.neu.edu/home/yiannis/dance/history.html

Northeastern University provides information on the history of ballet.

New York City Ballet

http://www.nycballet.com/nycb/home/

The official site of the New York City Ballet, founded in 1948 by George Balanchine and Lincoln Kirstein

San Francisco Ballet

www.sfballet.org

The official site of the San Francisco Ballet, founded in 1933, features information about one of the leading dance companies in the world.

All About Ballet

www.the-ballet.com

This general site provides information about ballet, the history of ballet, the genre's top performers, and the ballets themselves.

VIDEOGRAPHY

Balanchine, 156 minutes, Kultur Video, 2004, DVD. Starring George Balanchine.

Baryshnikov Live at Wolf Trap, 76 minutes, Kultur Video, 2004, DVD. Starring Mikhail Baryshnikov, Gelsey Kirkland, Marianna Tcherkassky.

Billy Elliot, prod. by Jon Finn and Greg Brenman, dir. by Stephen Daldry, 110 minutes, Universal Studios, 2000, DVD. Starring Jamie Bell.

Fonteyn and Nureyev: The Perfect Partnership, prod. and dir. by Peter Batty, 90 minutes, 1988, DVD. Starring Margot Fonteyn and Rudolf Nureyev.

The Glory of the Bolshoi, prod. by Julia Matheson and Carl Simons, 96 minutes, 1995, DVD. Starring dancers of the Bolshoi Ballet.

Great Pas de Deux, 111 minutes, Kultur Video, 2004, DVD. Starring Mikhail Baryshnikov, Margot Fonteyn, Rudolf Nureyev, Royal Ballet.

The New York City Ballet Workout, prod. and dir. by Richard Blanshard, 90 minutes, Palm Pictures, 2000, DVD.

Tchaikovsky: Swan Lake (Matthew Bourne), prod. by Bob Lockyear, Fiona Morris, James Wills, John Kelleher, Katharine Doré; dir. by Peter Mumford. 113 minutes, NVC Arts, 2000, DVD. Starring Adam Cooper.

The Video Dictionary of Classical Ballet, prod. and dir. by Robert Beck, 270 minutes, 1985, DVD. Featuring Merrill Ashley, Denis Jackson, Kevin McKenzie, and Georgina Parkinson.

PICTURE CREDITS

INDEX

ABOUT THE AUTHOR
AND CONSULTING EDITOR

Robin Rinaldi studied ballet for 10 years and taught it as a young adult. As a journalist, she has reviewed dance for the *Sacramento News & Review*, *Philadelphia Weekly,* and *7x7 Magazine* in San Francisco. She has interviewed such noted choreographers as Mark Morris, Ron Cunningham, David Parsons, and Judith Jamison. She is currently executive editor of *7x7 Magazine* in San Francisco, where she lives.

Consulting editor **Elizabeth A. Hanley** is Associate Professor Emerita of Kinesiology at the Pennsylvania State University. She holds a BS in physical education from the University of Maryland and an MS in physical education from Penn State, where she taught such courses as modern dance, figure skating, international folk dance, square and contra dance, and ballroom dance. She is the founder and former director of the Penn State International Dance Ensemble and has served as the coordinator of the dance workshop at the International Olympic Academy, in Olympia, Greece.